*For David and Paul*

# MENTORING AND

# DEVELOPING PRACTICE

# IN PRIMARY SCHOOLS

Supporting student teacher

learning in schools

**Anne Edwards and Jill Collison**

**Open University Press**
Buckingham • Philadelphia

Open University Press
Celtic Court
22 Ballmoor
Buckingham
MK18 1XW

and

1900 Frost Road, Suite 101
Bristol, PA 19007, USA

First Published 1996

A catalogue record of this book is available from the British Library

ISBN   0 335 19566 0 (hb)   0 335 19565 2 (pb)

*Library of Congress Cataloging-in-Publication Data*
Edwards, Anne, 1946–
    Mentoring and developing practice in primary schools : supporting
student teacher learning in schools / Anne Edwards and Jill
Collison.
      p.  cm.
    Includes bibliographical references and index.
    ISBN 0–335–19566–0 (hb), — ISBN 0–335–19565–2 (pbk.)
    1. Mentoring in education—Great Britain.   2. Master teachers
—Great Britain.   3. Student teaching—Great Britian.   I. Collison,
Jill, 1955– .   II. Title.
LB1731.4.E39   1996
370'.7'33—dc20                            96–11910
                                                  CIP

Typeset by Graphicraft Typesetters Ltd, Hong Kong
Printed in Great Britain by St Edmundsbury Press Ltd,
Bury St Edmunds, Suffolk

# MENTORING AND

# DEVELOPING PRACTICE

# IN PRIMARY SCHOOLS

# CONTENTS

# FIGURES AND TABLES

## Figures

## Tables

# ACKNOWLEDGEMENTS

First of all our thanks go to the mentors and students who generously not only tolerated the presence of (often) two researchers in their classrooms but also collaborated with us in the collection of data and the checking of ideas. We have anonymized all examples in the text. We would also like to thank particularly Carolyn Horne for making the project possible and for her continued support.

Jill Collison worked as research fellow on the project for three years and carried out the fieldwork. Anne Edwards was the project director. Both of them undertook analysis of the data. Others involved in data collection and analysis for the purposes of reliability were Jill Bundy, Katherine Edwards, Salah Elhassan, Jo Knox, Janice Neal and Sam Twiselton. David Webb read drafts of the text and made helpful comments. We are indebted to them all.

The book grew out of three years of conversations about the data between the authors. When writing Jill Collison took the lead on Chapter 4, identified many of the illustrative examples throughout the text and commented extensively on other chapters. Chapter 5 was written jointly and Anne Edwards wrote the remaining chapters.

# SECTION I

# FRAMEWORKS AND THEMES

## What is it all about?

What is the most important part of the work of teachers in primary schools? If you are a teacher, whether you are mainly a classteacher or mainly a manager, the continued well-being of the children in your school is likely to be central to your answer. For many of the children, caring for their well-being will be a matter of making sure they are doing as well as they might as they are helped through the curriculum. For some children, teachers' concerns will be primarily about their emotional or physical development. Indeed, for the majority of children, teachers will be concerning themselves with the delicate interplay between all three elements of the progress of young children at school. On top of that complexity, if you are a classteacher, you will have to create a climate and rhythm of activity in your classroom which ensures that the various needs of children are met and that your time is used well. Primary teaching is a complex activity and is not easily done.

Into the finely balanced system that is the well-run primary classroom comes a new figure. A student teacher arrives and is eager to teach in the classroom. Another set of needs have now to be met. But this newcomer is harder to assimilate into the well-established systems than a new child would be. In addition, the paperwork that explains what students now have to do makes it clear that classteachers are not just people who are generously providing the opportunity for students to try out ideas in their teaching spaces. Rather, they are mentors. The students are expected to learn a lot from their mentors while they are in school. What does all this entail? How will mentors be able to cope and still give priority to the children? How will they be able to meet the needs of the students? What on earth does being a mentor actually mean?

This is the question to be tackled throughout the book. Mentoring is an activity that changes in response to what students need, the possibilities available within particular schools or partnership arrangements and the way that mentors like to work.

Definitions of mentoring are evolving continuously. Some might even say that they are being continuously contested by those involved in initial teacher training. In this book we want to see mentoring as a developing concept. By taking that view we can try to place teacher-mentors at the centre of the construction of their own sense of what mentoring can and might be. We therefore want to direct the book towards the needs of teacher-mentors and to ask mentors to work with us in a process of understanding and testing ideas about effective mentoring.

Who then are the mentors? Different teacher training programmes will have different titles and different expectations for those involved in supporting the learning of student teachers in schools. Nevertheless there seem to be two main functions that are loosely covered by the title of mentor. One is more managerial than the other and we hope that the content of the book will be of direct relevance to mentors who are taking on any combination of those functions.

The more managerial role is often one of mentor of mentors in a school and may include the maintenance of links with a university. It is also likely to involve attention to the general welfare of the student teachers in the school. It will very probably include responsibility for creating a programme of student experience in school and demand considerable involvement in the final assessment of student performance. The less managerial aspect of mentoring relates to the role of mentor as teacher and supporter of student teachers as they work in classrooms with children. This element of mentoring will involve mentors in planning and evaluating the teaching of students alongside the students, in ways that will support the learning of students. One theme in the book is that this aspect of the role in fact involves more than planning and evaluating. It will include modelling practice, teaching alongside students and highlighting aspects of the students' own learning.

We are also aware that readers will be coming to this text from a range of training programmes. At this point we shall simply recognize that the work of mentors may involve total responsibility for the introduction of trainee teachers to professional knowledge. It may on the other hand constitute a fairly minimal role which is little different from simply providing a classroom for students' practical learning.

Much will depend upon the degree of responsibility for training agreed by a school and upon the support structures available through, for example, relationships with higher education. Consequently we are making no assumptions about the structures that underpin the mentoring demands made upon schools and individual teachers. Rather we are offering ways of understanding and developing the practices of mentoring that can be best developed to suit the needs of the trainees, the mentors and the schools in which mentoring is occurring. We shall be drawing on information from a study of initial teacher training in primary schools. However we believe that many of the aspects of the work we shall discuss are also relevant to mentors who are working with newly qualified teachers.

## Using the book

This text is meant to be a guide and stimulus for teachers who are also mentors. We are not offering a critique of school-based training and its origins. Rather we are accepting that there are advantages and difficulties for everyone involved in providing initial teacher training in primary schools. We shall take many of the advantages for granted and shall focus particularly on how you might deal with the difficulties that we and others have identified in our research into mentoring in primary schools.

In our discussion of mentoring we shall take as starting points the data we gathered during a three-year study of a degree programme which had training partnerships with primary schools at its core. We are not, however, just offering an account of one school-based training programme. Like many first attempts at this complex area, the programme we examined had several flaws. We will, however, draw on information we gathered over our three-year detailed examination of the experiences of students as they were trained in schools, in order to open up explorations of some of the challenges of mentoring and how they might be met.

Our data are rich and tell a fascinating story of how mentors have managed to make school-based training work and at what point they have felt they wished to draw a line under their responsibilities. We gathered the information in interviews, questionnaires, observations and recordings of conversations between mentors and students. We shall draw on these sources as we consider what is involved in mentoring but we are well aware that each programme and indeed each mentor will bring fresh perspectives to what being a mentor actually involves. We therefore expect readers to be data-gatherers too. We want to encourage mentors to collect information on their work as mentors and discuss it in the light of ideas we shall be putting forward.

The chapters in the book make up three linked sections which are planned so that the idea of mentoring may be first of all unpacked and secondly tested in schools against evidence that is gathered there. Finally we shall attempt to embed mentoring in ideas about healthy and effective schools. The first section of the book consists of Chapters 1 and 2 which explore ways of seeing both mentoring in initial teacher training and the learning of novice teachers. Section II consists of Chapters 3 to 8 and draws on case study material from our examination of mentoring for initial teacher training in primary schools. The final four chapters make up Section III and take the focus to staff development, school improvement, related quality assurance issues and ways forward for mentoring. In particular in Chapter 11 we suggest ways of making the most of relationships with higher education.

Being a mentor is a demanding role and a great deal has been written on the topic. We will not decorate our discussion with a lot of references. But at the end of every chapter you will find suggestions for further reading which will enable you to follow certain themes in greater depth. In addition, at the end of each chapter in Section II we provide some ideas for activities that groups of mentors might like to try as part of a staff development programme.

Tying the three sections of the book together is a view of teacher-mentors as sceptical practitioners who take nothing for granted but wish to test the ideas put forward in texts of this type in the realities of their working lives. We therefore offer the possibilities for action that arise from our study very tentatively for scrutiny.

We expect that readers will want to work from evidence and not rhetoric and will want to see their own evidence as valued as it deserves to be. Therefore we suggest that one way of using the book is to read Sections I and III so that common frameworks are established and meanings shared and clarified. Then use Section II, chapter by chapter, as starting points for some form of professional development programme. Such a programme might be individual learning but we would argue that there is a lot to be gained from seeing the activities as part of a paired or, better still, staff group endeavour in which the needs of the school become a major concern.

Mentoring for us is therefore more than just what goes on between expert and novice to lead the novice into professional expertise. Indeed, we are distinctly unhappy about definitions of mentoring in initial teacher training that result in mentors and students or newly qualified teachers being *desert-islanded* in the ocean of school life. Rather we prefer to see mentoring as one important element in the dynamics of a developing school. We are not sure that the potential for staff and school development is always evident in discussions of mentoring, which all too often have been written by higher education tutors who are themselves marooned in a particular phase of teacher development.

Clearly we are taking as a given that effective mentors can first develop and then survive only in schools that allow that to happen. That is, that new professional roles and opportunities can only be created in schools that are themselves able to develop to accommodate the demands and advantage of these new roles. In Chapter 10 we pay particular attention to how developing schools are able to incorporate and make the most of what these new roles have to offer as a whole-school endeavour.

## The contexts for active mentoring

Mentoring is a feature of training in many organizations in the 1990s. It is used primarily to induct newcomers into the expectations and procedures that operate in a specific workplace. It is therefore often an important element in the induction of a new recruit into the way that a particular organization operates. While this aspect of mentoring may be relevant in part to the mentoring of newly qualified teachers, mentoring in initial teacher training is much more than that. Frequently mentors have to take responsibility for teaching student teachers key aspects of their professional training curriculum and recognize that they are preparing students to work eventually in other schools. Mentoring in initial teacher training is consequently an active process which makes considerable demands on teacher-mentors as it has to lead to students being able to understand quite broad principles of teaching and learning.

To that end mentoring will, for example, involve mentors in contriving situations in which a teacherly form of mentoring can take place. In Section II we shall look at the details of the contexts for mentoring, contrived and otherwise, in school. These contexts will include mentoring conversations between mentors and students (Chapter 3), mentoring while teaching (Chapter 4), and school-based seminars (Chapter 5). These situations will not always occur naturally and, as we point out in Chapter 2, students may not always be eager to be seen as learners who require the teacherly help of mentors. Mentoring as a consequence involves careful management of the contexts of student teacher learning.

An emphasis on the contexts for learning is central to the book. As we pursue the idea first of students and then of teachers and tutors as learners in schools, we do not see learning as a simple *within-person set of processes* which are merely enabled by a sympathetic context. Rather we recognize a *constant and creative interaction between learners and contexts*. In the case of teacher training in schools the meanings of teaching and learning are constantly created, negotiated and tested by those who are acting and therefore learning in the contexts. We shall argue that these contexts also benefit from ensuring that those who are in a position to question underlying assumptions are given ready access to the negotiation of meanings in context.

## Models of mentoring in initial teacher training

Mentoring for us is, in part, a form of teaching and needs to be planned in the same way as the teaching of pupils. Although being a friend and counsellor are important features of mentoring they are only the starting points from which a sound teacherly mentoring relationship can develop. We shall elaborate these ideas in Chapter 2. But first let us look at what research on being a mentor in primary schools is already telling us about mentoring there.

Maynard and Furlong (1993) in the context of their work on school-based training have identified three possible mentor functions. These they describe as: mentor as model and interpreter; as instructor; and as co-enquirer. According to Maynard and Furlong these ways of interacting with trainees will depend upon where in his or her own cycle of learning a student is. We shall argue that the learning of student teachers in classrooms has to be carefully supported, particularly in its early stages, for their sake as well as for the sake of the pupils. The amount of support may be subsequently reduced as students achieve a basic confidence and competence in some areas. Later, as students develop their professional repertoires of action and wider competence, mentors can begin to work with students in order to enable them to think in informed ways about their practice, its development and its wider implications for the lives of children.

Russell and Munby (1991) in their work in high schools in North America go further than just suggesting that teacher-mentors support informed student reflection on practice. They propose the joint exploration of *puzzles in practice* by students and their mentors as a way of opening up professional practice to mutual examination by student teachers and their mentors. We shall be looking at action research a little later in this chapter and in more detail in Chapter 9. Frameworks offered by action research may provide a useful way into the exploration of puzzles in practice. This approach can be both exciting and quite threatening for students and for mentors. Seeking out problematics does not suit everyone and needs careful management. Certainty is something that most students seek avidly.

Another related question we shall be raising in later chapters is the importance of a match between individual students' learning needs and what different styles of mentoring can provide. In our three-year study of mentoring in primary schools we found that the mentors we observed and talked with could be placed on a continuum which was rather like that identified by Maynard and Furlong. The functions we found were labelled carer, guide and challenger. But the continuum did not appear to relate to where the students were in their development as teachers. Rather it was connected to how individual mentors wished to describe and act out their roles in relation to a training partnership with one higher education institution and to the priority they gave the mentor role amidst the many competing demands on their time (Collison and Edwards, 1994).

We found that all the mentors in the study regarded themselves as carers who wished to make life as manageable as possible for the student teachers in their classrooms and particularly to provide safe places for the trial and error learning of the trainees. Some saw their role as more than that and as offering structured advice in joint planning sessions and making suggestions during evaluations of recent lessons. A small minority were helping the student teachers to consider past actions critically by challenging them to think of other ways they might have worked with the children. Our data did seem to indicate that, for example, if a teacher was a challenger, she or he was acting in that way quite early in the relationship with the students and that some of the mentors never did more than show a concern for the students and their classrooms as places in which students could try out ideas.

What our data suggest is that mentoring is not an instinctive activity which can be carried out by good practitioners as another layer of their professional function as classteachers. Rather our findings tell us that mentoring consists of a set of skills that have to be learnt; that there is a knowledge base to teacher training into which mentors themselves need to be inducted; and that teachers will act as mentors to the extent that they understand the possibilities or limits of the role in their particular situation.

## Students as learners

The position of students as learners in schools forms a major theme in the book. The framework for our examination is set up in Chapter 2 and it informs our discussions throughout Section II. Our starting point is that students are often reluctant to see themselves as learners in school and prefer to be recognized as effective operators. This analysis presents major challenges for mentors who as a consequence have to set quite clear groundrules for their relationships with students. These points are discussed in Chapters 2, 3, 4 and 5. In Chapter 6 we examine the importance of students' acquisition of curriculum subject knowledge as a precursor to the development of their task-setting skills. In Chapter 7 we tackle some of the major principles of practice through which students can begin to make sense of their own practices and connect them to the more widely held principles available in the professional and research literature.

However, throughout the book we emphasize that students' learning has to stem from more than an analysis of their own practices. Indeed the student as reflective practitioner is barely mentioned in the text. This is not because we believe that students should not consider their own practices with self-critical eyes. Rather we want to emphasize the development of thinking practitioners. Thinking practitioners in our definition are able to connect their analyses of what goes on in schools with the frameworks that are available in the professional and research literature.

We therefore recognize that students will develop as teachers throughout their training and into their careers as teachers. In our discussions of student development we are aware of the different aspects or levels of training that students might experience as they pursue their training. These aspects were summarized by Furlong *et al.* (1988), in the period before the implementation of school-centred training or training partnerships, as follows.

- *Level (a) direct practice*
  Practical training through direct experience in schools and classrooms.

- *Level (b) indirect practice*
  'Detached' training in practical matters usually [in 1988] conducted in classes and workshops in training institutions.
- *Level (c) practical principles*
  Critical study of the principles of practice and their use.
- *Level (d) disciplinary theory*
  Critical study of practice and its principles in the light of fundamental theory and research.

(1988:132)

The demands of Circular 14/93 (DFE, 1993) for the training of primary school teachers through an enhanced role for schools place a different perspective on these levels, in England and Wales at least. One response is to consider the extent to which these areas of student experience may be addressed in schools. This is the line we follow in the book. At the same time we suggest that these new demands on schools may warrant a revisiting of the relationship between schools and universities that may be to the benefit of both. This idea is picked up particularly in Chapter 11 where we suggest what higher education might have to offer schools.

We are also aware that students move through stages of confidence and competence. We touch upon competence in Chapter 8 when we consider the assessment responsibilities of mentors. In addition we find Maynard and Furlong's 1993 analysis of student progress a useful reminder of the concerns of students as they start to learn to teach. Maynard and Furlong suggest that students progress through five stages. These they describe as:

- early idealism
- survival
- recognizing the difficulties
- hitting the plateau
- moving on.

These stages alert us to the simple idealism of students as they start to learn to teach and the preconceptions of teaching that they bring with them. They remind us that learning to teach is a public activity and failure is to be avoided at all costs. Dealing with complexity of teaching is something that has to be tackled, but it has to be managed in ways that allow students to continue to learn confidently from their experiences. The plateau is a familiar feature of learning to teach. Having found something that works, students want to stick to it and avoid the risk involved in developing their practice. Some students do move on to focus quite clearly on pupil learning and manage interventions to support that. However it is very clear that those who do it well are in a minority and that the status of newly qualified teacher provides an important period for further development. To summarize Maynard and Furlong, learning to be a teacher is more than merely learning to teach. It is a complex and frequently threatening process that has to be carefully managed by those whose job it is to support student development.

### Learning to mentor

We shall be arguing in Chapter 2 that *learning by doing* is only part of the students' learning process. We emphasize that learners need goals and that they need a variety of forms of guidance from more expert members of the community. Yet in most cases mentors are thrust into the new role of mentoring with only the most meagre guidance. Mentors are often left to manage their own learning; in other words they do have to learn by doing, and to take on mentoring as just one more facet of a varied set of functions that have come to include, for example, curriculum management and pupil assessment. We hope that this book will be of some help, but it will not provide a set of tips on how to mentor. What it will do is set an agenda for the development of the skills and conceptual base of mentoring. In order to use that agenda to direct their own professional development, mentors will need to test some of the ideas in their own practices.

If you are a mentor and operating as an independent learner you may find it helpful to have a framework for that testing. We shall elaborate the framework we are suggesting in Chapter 9. However at this point we think that it would be useful for you to consider how you might evaluate your practice in ways that can support you as you become a more expert mentor and can help you as you work with and guide the learning of student teachers.

The framework that we suggest here is a simple one and will probably be familiar. It is the evaluation cycle that runs through four questions. These are:

- Where are we now?
- Where do we want to get to?
- How will we get there?
- How will we know when we have got there?

These questions imply diagnosis, goal setting, planning, and evaluation against the goals that were set. Let us think about them in relation to student learning. We can translate them into questions regarding what students already understand about an area of their teacher training curriculum, for example how to manage a whole-class discussion; what they need to understand next as beginning teachers; how you might provide the opportunities for them to acquire and consolidate their new understandings; and whether they did. Alongside that sequence will be a concern to evaluate just how well you managed to provide appropriate learning experiences and support.

We suggest that you keep in mind the framework we have just given as you work through the book. The focus on student learning and their curricular goals will sometimes be hard to maintain as students often don't want to be seen as learners in classrooms. The focus on your own learning may be even more of a challenge on top of all other demands made upon you. Yet we suggest that you do try to hang on to it.

One way of managing the focus on your own performance may be through the use of a reflective diary. We are not suggesting assiduous recording of every event. Rather we suggest that you use the diary as an *aide memoire* that allows you sometimes to record the intended focus of student teacher learning; what they did; what you did; and how well both sets of actions worked in relation to the focus. The evaluation of effectiveness might also take into account the impact on the pupils of the actions of all the adults involved.

We suggest the following format for a reflective diary. Take a smallish notebook and use the left-hand page for noting down what happened during a session in which you were acting as mentor. It might be, for example, a joint teaching session or a planning conversation. Then use the right-hand page for identifying perhaps two areas. The first could be where you want to go next with the student. The second could be reflections on your own actions and how you might have acted or interacted differently with the student. Information in the notebook can subsequently form the basis of a discussion with other mentors about the development of mentoring practices. We are certainly not suggesting that diary-keeping goes on every day, but there may be certain features of mentor practice which you would like to work on as you read this book.

We are believers in the power of evidence as a starting point for considered examination of practice and of the need for teachers to be the people who collect evidence on their own practices. We also believe that talking about what you are doing with other mentors will help the development of practice by clarifying what is involved. You will see in Chapter 2 that we emphasize the importance of language use to learning. The evidence that you collect can help to ensure that discussions with fellow mentors about mentoring maintain a focus on the practice of mentoring and its implications.

## The purposes of school-based training

If we look at what the stakeholders in school-based training appear to want from the exercise it is easy to construct a picture of mentoring as a conservative force. Our data tell us very clearly that schools want minimum disruption as a result of increased participation in teacher training. The priorities of schools and teachers understandably remain the achievement of their pupils. University tutors simply need partnership programmes to work so that their quality assurance systems are not found wanting. Students want to be able to perform effectively in classrooms and don't want their lives in school made too complicated. The Government certainly wants training to emphasize the acquisition of the craft knowledge of teaching. None of these interests indicates that initial teacher training in schools is to provide a radical learning experience for students. Neither is it to have much impact on the schools in which it takes place.

Yet there are alternative ways of seeing school-based initial training and we touch on some of them in Chapters 10 and 11. There we advocate a 'reperceiving' (Senge, 1994) of initial training and its potential for supporting school improvement strategies. We draw in part on the ideas that lie behind the Professional Development School movement in North America. We particularly stress that Professional Development Schools require quite considerable shifts of emphasis in the ways that universities conduct their relationships with schools.

## Education as a common enterprise

A strong assumption behind this book therefore is the belief that education is a continuum that runs from the experience of nursery school children, through higher education to the professional development of all practitioners whether based in schools or universities. There are specialisms within the continuum, but the potential for collaborative action in line with a common set of purposes is something to be recognized and aimed at. This set of purposes or vision is necessarily value-laden and open to continuous debate and reframing but we argue that the power to debate and reframe should rest within the remit of all participants wherever they are based. If this view is accepted then partnership in initial teacher training can be seen as only one element in a process of continuous learning and renewal of understanding about the learning of children, of beginning teachers and of expert practitioners.

In this book we focus particularly on the primary education phase of the continuum and suggest that primary education is a coherent community of practice. In discussing communities of practice in Chapter 2 we look at the work of Jean Lave (Lave and Wenger, 1991; Chaiklin and Lave, 1993). We focus particularly on her notion of a community of practice as a field in which knowledge is located and developed by those who participate in that community. We suggest that all who are involved in enhancing the learning opportunities of children in primary schools are members of a specific community of practice and need to work together.

Participants in the community of practice of primary education include classteachers, senior managers in schools, student teachers, non-teaching assistants, higher education tutors and researchers. Indeed we see school-based initial teacher training to be an important opportunity for the scrutiny and development of the practice of primary school teaching.

## Further reading

There are some excellent collections of papers on initial teacher training and mentoring available. Teacher training is a lively research area in North America and Northern Europe. Keeping up to date can be daunting. The following academic journals are well worth searching: *Journal of Education for Teaching* (Carfax); *Teachers and Teaching: theory and practice* (Carfax) and *Teaching and Teacher Education* (Pergamon). All of these contain analyses of research into teaching, teacher training and continuing professional education that are of a high standard and from across the world. *Mentoring and Tutoring* (Trentham Books) is a useful journal which often carries summaries of more extensive UK research projects and work in progress in the development of mentoring and tutoring.

There are a number of interesting collections of papers on initial teacher training in general and training in schools in particular. However, those that focus on primary education are few and far between. None of the texts we shall list in this section takes a specifically primary school focus but all contain papers that make up a sound basis for further study of teacher training for primary phase specialists.

Calderhead, J. and Gates, P. (eds) (1993) *Conceptualising Reflection in Teacher Development*, London, Falmer, provides a very good basis for an exploration of the issues in teacher education just prior to the introduction of training partnerships in England and Wales, and draws on UK and North American studies.

Wilkin, M. (ed.) (1992) *Mentoring in Schools*, London, Kogan Page, and McIntyre, D., Hagger, H. and Wilkin, M. (eds) (1993) *Mentoring: Perspectives on School-Based Teaching Education*, London, Kogan Page, draw mainly on UK research and contain excellent sets of papers which lay the groundwork for much of current understandings of mentoring in Britain.

Reid, I., Constable, H. and Griffiths, R. (eds) (1994) *Teacher Education Reform: Current Research*, London, Paul Chapman, contains 26 short and often highly informative papers. The majority report evaluations of first attempts at school-based training. The perspectives of both schools and universities are found in the contributions.

McBride, R. (ed.) (1995) *Teacher Education Policy: Some Issues Arising from Research and Practice*, London, Falmer, is an interesting and wide-ranging collection of papers which places current changes in training practices within the policy frameworks examined by researchers. The starting points for considering the implications of policy for practice include philosophy, student teacher learning and professional development, action research, school improvement and continuing professional development.

Furlong, J. and Maynard, T. (1995) *Mentoring Student Teachers*, London, Routledge, is not an edited collection and has more of a focus on training in primary schools than do the other texts listed. Drawing on the research of the authors, it provides an informative analysis of the processes of mentoring and is in many ways complementary to this text. For example it foregrounds details of recent changes in government policies for the training of teachers and explores stages in the development of students as teachers in classrooms.

# STUDENTS AS

# LEARNERS

## The purpose of this chapter

As you will have already gathered from the previous chapter, student learning is the major theme of this book. It will therefore be no surprise to discover that we see this chapter to be the key to most of those that follow. It is here that we shall attempt to lay out the framework for mentoring and for student learning that will underpin what we discuss in later chapters. We shall be emphasizing the importance of structuring learning experiences, the relationships that exist between language and learning and the crucial role of teachers in assisting the learning of novices. What is perhaps new is that we are now suggesting that these understandings are applied systematically by mentors as they assist the learning of the students who are learning to teach in their classrooms.

## What is there to learn?

This chapter could be a book in its own right and this section a fairly weighty chapter within the book. Consequently we have been selective while at the same time recognizing that a great deal has been written about student learning in and out of classrooms. If we were to ask student teachers as they start their training what it is they need to learn the answer would be 'to teach'. Clearly successful performance in the classroom is a priority. A large number of students enter their training with very strong pictures in their minds of what kinds of teacher they want to be and how they will act in classrooms.

These images are drawn from their own experiences of school, and often specifically of primary school, some time in the past. Their pictures are based on being a learner in the classroom and the quality of relationship they experienced with the teachers they liked. As a result students are frequently oriented towards the creation of good relationships with pupils but have a considerably less clear idea about children as learners, the nature of the curriculum and the management of time and space that is at the centre of creating conditions for pupil learning. They have equally little notion of schools as organizations and the distinct roles as, for example, curriculum coordinators, that many classteachers carry alongside their main roles.

One of the first topics to be tackled with students in teacher training programmes is therefore: what does being a teacher mean for you? This kind of diagnosis is essential if trainers are to work with and support the learning and development of the students in their care. Students, however, are often impatient and want to leap into teaching. Were they to do that the majority would become rapidly unstuck and demoralized.

At this point the trainer has to take control and try to slow down and pace the students' induction into the processes of teaching. One way of doing this is to find a focus for student learning and to allow students time for precise observation and detailed discussion of related activities before moving them to the planning and the undertaking of small-scale teaching interventions initially with a limited number of children. These interventions should each be followed by mentoring conversations which relate actions to student learning goals.

The stages we have just outlined make up a cycle of teaching and learning that will be familiar to everyone who works with children in primary schools. Firstly we called attention to what student teachers appear to be bringing with them when they enter their training. Then we considered how student expectations and understandings matched the goals they would have to achieve if they were to become qualified teachers. Finally we proposed the beginnings of a structured programme of learning that ensured that students first recognized the goals of their learning and then engaged in carefully structured experiences that were designed to enable them to learn what they needed to. The discussions that we suggested should be placed after the activity are central to the learning process. We shall consistently stress that aspects of student learning can be highlighted in these discussions and that it is there that students' unintended learning can be recognized and developed.

Most teacher trainers will perhaps criticize the clarity of the teaching and learning cycle for students we have just outlined. The reality is that all too often the demands of classroom experience mean that students focus only on what is happening with the pupils and pay scant attention to their own learning in classrooms. We recognize that shifting attention from pupil learning to student learning is the main challenge of mentoring in primary schools.

So what do students learn while they are in primary school classrooms? One major argument claims that what they acquire is an understanding of the particular kind of knowledge that is put into action by expert teachers as they work with the unpredictability of classroom life. This is a form of *knowledge in action* that is extremely difficult to articulate.

To explore the difficulty of talking about this kind of knowledge, just consider one small decision you made in interaction with a child or group of children the last time you taught. What did you take into account in that decision? We can only begin to imagine, but would assume it would include previous interactions related to the focus of your decision, your immediate and longer-term intentions related to pupil learning and perhaps the use of resources, what other children were doing and how they might react, and many other factors. These would all draw on your own well-developed, if perhaps little discussed, view of how you can best enhance the learning of these particular children in this classroom. Teasing out all the elements in the decision you made is not easy and certainly not something that is a regular part of classroom life! Shulman in 1987 talked about the kind of knowledge we have just described as an *amalgam* of knowledge of what is to be taught, knowledge of how to manage children's learning in classrooms and knowledge of how best to teach. He describes this knowledge as the special province of teachers. The amalgam occurs because these elements are so often called into play at the same time in teacher decision making. However once they become an amalgam they are difficult to pull apart and discuss separately.

The importance of student teachers acquiring this kind of teacher knowledge presents particular problems. First, knowledge that directs action when taking action is difficult to talk about. If this kind of knowledge is reduced to a series of tips, it simplifies the decision making in ways that do not take into account the fact that so many teacher decisions are reactive and creative in the complex contexts that are classrooms. Secondly, it suggests that teacher knowledge can only be accessed by engaging in teaching and in experiencing the use of that knowledge for oneself. A consequence of this is that experience of teaching is seen to be central to the knowledge acquisition of students. But it is very difficult to find ways of talking beforehand about the reactive and creative thinking that is to be put into action, consolidating the knowledge it represents after the teaching event, or even checking what the action meant for the students. All of these difficulties have to be faced in the mentoring relationship.

## What do we know about student learning?

We already know that students are trying to learn something quite difficult. They have to acquire a set of skills that are informed by their understanding of, among other things, the dynamics of classroom life, a coherent view of children and how they learn, an understanding of the curriculum to be learnt by the children, and knowledge of how to support the learning of children on a curriculum in a complex and variable setting. The relationship between knowledge of what is involved in teaching and the skill of effective teaching is crucial if we are to recognize the complexity of teaching. We believe that we need to see teaching as more than a craft that can be acquired, like weaving, by being a watchful apprentice who learns how to produce regular patterns. Though there must be times when we have all wished that a primary classroom could have the predictable qualities of a loom!

When talking about a skill like teaching we are often tempted to see the elements of *knowledge about* and *knowledge how* as quite distinct. We have heard it said quite frequently that knowledge about teaching is of little value and what really counts is classroom performance. The people to say this most often are the students themselves, who come into their training so impatient to be teachers. As we said earlier in this chapter, expert teachers are, however, operating with an amalgam of elements of knowledge about teaching and are turning that knowledge into effective practice as they act in classrooms.

An easy answer to dealing with these two kinds of knowledge in teacher training is to say that one is the responsibility of universities and the other is the responsibility of schools. This may be true up to a point. But we believe strongly that in teacher education these two kinds of knowledge need to be kept in close contact for two important reasons. First, knowledge about teaching can only be developed in ways that are relevant to the improvement of education if it develops out of the needs and insights of the whole education community and is developed and tested in that community. Secondly, our understanding of the relationship between understanding and skill, which owes a lot to Tomlinson (1995) and Tomlinson and Saunders (1995), tells us that the complex skill of teaching is an informed skill and not simply a string of unthinkingly applied procedures. The amalgam of teacher knowledge that we described earlier is therefore crucial to good quality practice.

So how do we pull together these two kinds of knowledge and perhaps find mutually supportive ways for schools and higher education to work to ensure the learning of student teachers? This question does not have an easy answer. We need to consider how student teachers learn, what the various sites on which they learn have to offer them at different times and how those who come into contact with them in the various places in which they learn give them the help they need when they need it.

## Assisting learning

The ideas in the last paragraph indicate that learning is a process which requires support. We shall therefore start with a teaching and learning cycle and acknowledge that we are being selective in what we present. The learning cycle we shall discuss was partially outlined in the first section of this chapter and is the set of processes that underpins much of primary school practice (Edwards, 1994a; Edwards and Knight, 1994). It can be seen in the often-used lesson plan of the introduction, by a teacher to a large group, of new language, ideas and ways of approaching an activity. The introduction is followed by structured small group work or paired work aimed at encouraging children to move towards understanding of the new ideas and the use of the language in which the ideas are carried. Group work is then followed by a more demanding task in which children put ideas and skills to use, perhaps in problem-solving. This activity may then be followed at a later date by a routine task in which pupils learn to incorporate the new ideas and skills into their repertoires of understanding and behaviour.

The cycle we have just outlined can be seen as a movement of learners from the public arena where teachers introduce, in public, what is accepted as publicly understood knowledge, into a semi-private and safe opportunity to grope towards individual understandings of that knowledge in small group or paired work. Later this experience is followed by the exercise of that knowledge in the public world where a teacher can check on the degree of understanding achieved and the learners can make contributions to the way that knowledge is framed and used in the public arena. The public–private difference we have just outlined draws on the work of Vygotsky and his followers both in the USSR earlier this century and more latterly in the UK and North America (see for example Tharp and Gallimore, 1988; Mercer, 1995).

The framework that these writers offer is based on Vygotsky's view that learning happens on two *planes*: the first he called the *intermental plane* (when information is heard and perhaps partially understood) and the second he termed the *intramental plane* (when information is fitted into an individual's current system for categorizing related information). The intermental plane is likely to operate in the public arena of, for example, a lecture where public understandings dominate. The intramental plane is more likely to be evident when a learner can explore tentative understandings in safe private or semi-private settings of, for example, small teacherless group work in a primary classroom. The intramental plane is where understandings are internalized and existing mental structures are adjusted in order to accommodate new information. Learning situations which aim to enable pupils to work at the intramental plane are the most difficult for teachers to contrive when planning for pupil learning. The difficulty is no less when planning for student learning.

One of the most important features of intramental plane learning is the opportunity for learners to use the relevant language so that the meanings associated with a particular set of ideas can be tested and clarified, often in conversation. Our interpretation of intramental plane learning is quite social. The intention is that the learner becomes more confident and comfortable with the meanings and the language. We shall be stressing that point when we discuss mentoring conversations in Chapter 3 and seminars in Chapter 5.

An important feature of activity at the intramental plane is the role of the person who takes responsibility both for inducting learners into publicly acceptable understandings and for developing the individual strengths of learners. In initial teacher training, taking this view of teaching and learning, a mentor as inductor supports or *scaffolds* the learning of a novice in a variety of ways until the novice is able to work without the support of the mentor. We shall return to the nature of scaffolding in classrooms later in this chapter when we look at whether or not mentors are actually teachers of students and in more detail in Chapter 7 where we examine aspects of pedagogy.

## The role of mentors in assisting student learning

An understanding of the work of Vygotsky and those who have developed his ideas is useful because the framework that underpins their view of learning can be closely related to an understanding of how trainers in different situations might support the learning of students. These situations might be lecture theatres, tutorial rooms, staff rooms or classrooms.

If we try to map the learning cycle we have just outlined, we can begin to trace the way that learners might progress from contact with the knowledge held by others to constructing their own understandings and then to putting those understandings into action. In Figures 2.1 and 2.2 we have attempted such a map, so that we can see how the places where students learn have a part to play in the way we think about teacher training and the roles of mentors as they work with students in schools.

Figure 2.1 represents the situation in training courses which do not see partnership between universities and schools to be a central feature of teacher training. It demonstrates a separation of theory and practice and a view of teacher training as the application in the classroom of externally acquired knowledge. If we trace the experience of students through the four quadrants in Figure 2.1 we can see distinctly different roles for the two training sites of schools and universities and those who work in them. We are of course presenting a simplification in order to illustrate a point.

Starting in quadrant A, students receive the theory of education in the university and in quadrant B they work towards an understanding of the educational principles involved in teaching and develop confidence in their knowledge about teaching. They then find themselves in quadrant C, where they have to apply that knowledge in practice in a classroom and find that it isn't that simple. This is the point when theory is rejected as irrelevant. They quickly learn all they can by observing what the classteachers do and they try to do the same. They survive. In quadrant D, back at the university, they try to make sense of it all in the language offered by educational theory and find that they cannot. Of course this is a parody. We can

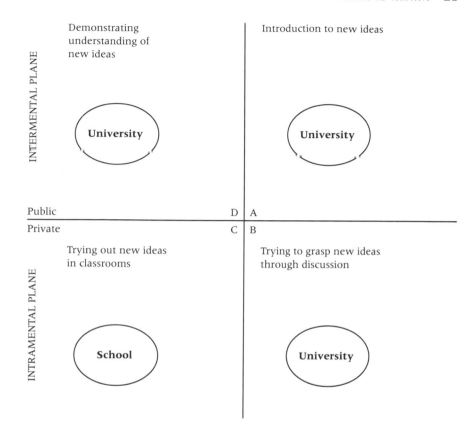

*Figure 2.1*   A Vygotskian framework for training without partnership

think of no training programmes that have operated exactly like that in the last 15 or so years. None the less, the potential for the fragmentation of the students' experiences remained in the days before enhanced cooperation between schools and universities.

In Figure 2.2 we have attempted to trace the movement of students through the situations provided for training in a programme, where there are stronger links between theory and practice. If you are not involved in a partnership scheme but have considerable school control of the training programme, the pathway will still be of relevance as, although the situations may perhaps differ a little, the processes will remain the same. A more detailed version of this model can be found in Edwards (1995a).

In Figure 2.2 students again move alphabetically through all four quadrants. In A they are introduced to key ideas in educational theory as these relate to classroom practice and also see examples of interesting practice in schools. In B they attempt to make sense of what they have heard, read

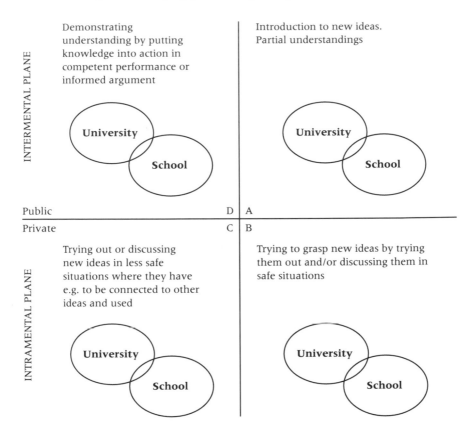

INTERMENTAL PLANE

Demonstrating
understanding by putting
knowledge into action in
competent performance or
informed argument

Introduction to new ideas.
Partial understandings

University

School

University

School

Public                                                    D | A
Private                                                   C | B

INTRAMENTAL PLANE

Trying out or discussing
new ideas in less safe
situations where they have
e.g. to be connected to other
ideas and used

Trying to grasp new ideas by trying
them out and/or discussing them in
safe situations

University

School

University

School

*Figure 2.2*    A Vygotskian framework for a training partnership

and seen in both school and university so that *knowledge about* teaching found in the university can be brought close to the *knowledge how* of teaching that was observed in a school. The sense-making may be assisted by finely focused observations or small-scale tightly structured teaching experiences.

In quadrant C students are, initially in their experience of teaching at least, placed in safe and well-structured classroom contexts to work out their ideas about teaching children an aspect of the curriculum. They work out these ideas in their planning and while actually teaching. This is where training becomes difficult and the important role of the mentors as conversationalists and guides for student learning becomes clear. Simply trying out ideas is not enough for students if the focus of the experience is to be the students' own learning. For students' learning to be consolidated we would argue that aspects of their experience need to be highlighted and connections to wider public meanings made. The highlighting can occur in conversations but, as we shall argue in Chapter 5, connections with wider frames of reference may more easily be made in planned seminars.

Quadrant D in Figure 2.2 is the final stage. That is reached when the students are confident and competent and able to demonstrate informed mastery of an aspect of teaching. One of the difficulties with school-based training is the temptation to see quadrants C and D as the same stage in the students' cycle of learning too early in their training. Of course most students, because of their impatience to be teachers, are all too ready to go along with this tendency and they try to present themselves immediately as competent teachers. For this reason too, students are often reluctant to spend too long standing back and looking at the quadrant B stage.

For the moment two main points arise from Figure 2.2, though we shall continue to return to it in later chapters. First, in each of the quadrants, in a partnership model of school-based training at least, learning occurs in both schools and universities in all four stages of the cycle. We would argue that this is important if we are to work towards thoughtful practice and a high-quality amalgam of well-informed teacher knowledge. Secondly, because both mentors and university tutors are involved in all four stages, support for students can be more immediately responsive to their needs as learners and can more easily accommodate differences in students' approaches to learning (Edwards, 1995a).

The model we have just outlined in Figure 2.2 also implies the need for clearly defined experiences for students which may not always involve teaching. They may, for example in quadrant B, involve focused observations of how children respond to a teacher's management strategies. Similarly small elements of practice may be identified, for example tidying-up time, and students can be asked to consider their own learning as they tackle those elements. We know that this is not easy in busy classrooms, but it is perhaps easier to achieve when we see students as learners in classrooms and not as teachers.

The cycle we have outlined in Figure 2.2 will operate many times for students as they progress through the training provided. Each small cycle can have a learning focus for students which will be based on their own starting points, the curriculum they are to follow in order to achieve their qualification and the opportunities available in the classrooms in which they are able to work.

At this point you might like to consider something that a student you know needs to learn. This could be something as general as how to manage a whole-class group or as specific as how to teach one-to-one correspondence to a small group of non-readers. Can you use Figure 2.2 to plan a set of learning experiences in school for the student? What would be the role of the university in a partnership arrangement? Where might additional help come from colleagues or others in the school? What will the student be learning at each stage in the cycle? How can mentoring assist that learning?

## Can you learn how to be an effective teacher simply by teaching?

By now we imagine that you will be able to gamble on our answer to that question being a fairly firm 'No, you cannot'. You will also probably recognize that we believe that classrooms are where students learn a lot about teaching and almost everything they can know about how to teach well themselves. The problem that we have emphasized is that students are often far too impatient to be teachers and as a consequence sometimes attend too little to their own learning needs and the need to acquire knowledge about teaching.

Students rarely seem to see themselves as learners in classrooms full of pupils. Our observations of students in classrooms and our analyses of mentoring conversations have told us that students tend to see themselves as polite guests in the classrooms of their host teachers. As we shall suggest in Chapter 3, they appear to be offering the tasks or activities for pupils that they bring with them as gifts for the teachers and their pupils, and they want the tasks to be implemented smoothly. They value the opportunity to use the sites for task implementation that their mentors provide but want to 'get in there' and efficiently carry out the activities they have planned in ways that don't upset the balance and rhythm of the class. They are after all the polite guests working in the sites that are owned and operated by their mentors.

When we add this picture of students in classrooms to the recognition that classrooms are very public places and not good situations for any risk of public failure we can perhaps see that allowing students to rush too quickly into teaching as *the way* of learning how to teach is to pay too little attention to their own needs as learners. However, they need quadrant A and B experiences and these need to be well paced.

The work of Jean Lave and her associates in the United States is particularly helpful as we begin to see how this gentle induction into skilful teaching might be achieved. (See for example Lave and Wenger, 1991; Chaiklin and Lave, 1993.) Lave and Wenger, in common with many of the UK perspectives on teacher training, take the idea of apprenticeship as a starting point for their examination of how skilful practice is achieved. But, as we have already argued, they believe that although apprenticeship is a place to begin, when you are looking at learning how to operate in a complex situation, simple comparisons with sitting-by-Nelly models of apprenticeship collapse. In addition we have already suggested that sitting by anyone is the last thing that impatient students want to do!

At the centre of Lave's work is the idea of learning as increasing participation in the *communities of practice* in which knowledge is located and created. The notion of a community of practice as a location and testing ground for ideas that are shared and used in that community is helpful. Lave and Wenger describe their perspective on the situated and social nature of knowledge and learning as follows:

the concept of situated activity . . . took on the proportions of a general theoretical perspective, the basis of claims about the relational character of knowledge and learning, about the negotiated character of meaning, and the concerned (engaged, dilemma-driven) nature of the learning activity for the people involved . . . the view that agent, activity and world mutually constitute each other.

(Lave and Wenger, 1991: 33)

This definition allows us to begin to move away from a simple separation of *knowledge about* and *knowledge how* when we think of learning to teach. A community of practice in which primary teacher knowledge is located may be, for example, a school. It is also arguably the profession of primary teaching and may include teachers and researchers in universities amongst others.

Communities of practice have value systems, give common meanings to particular forms of behaviour, have a shared history, are shaped by those who operate within them and in turn shape their participants and their understandings. Full participation in a community of practice implies the ability to read the subtle demands of the community and to contribute to the dynamics that are operating in it in order to play a part in its continuous development. It also means being able to use the language of that community in ways that have meaning for the participants within it. Using the language does not mean simply learning and applying established meanings, although that is part of the process, but also generating and testing new interpretations in the community of practice.

Being a classteacher is to play a major role as a full participant in the community of teacher practice that operates in a school. There may be times, however, when individual teachers are not operating as full participants in elements of the community of practice of a school. For example some may move more slowly than others towards the integration of new technologies into their classroom practices. They may start by offering technology-based tasks to pupils as limited activities and only cautiously bring them into the centre of their planning.

In this case we would be witnessing what Lave and Wenger describe as *peripheral participation*. It is, they argue, not a teaching technique but a way of looking at learning. Peripheral participation can be seen as an important stage in the induction of learners into confident and competent practice. Gradually learners move towards full participation. Once able to participate fully in that element of the community of practice, participants are in the position, through their actions and evaluations, to contribute to the development of understandings held by others in the community. Central to their view of a community of practice and the development of knowledge within it, is an acceptance that all members are learners who participate through their learning in the development of practices and the ways that they are understood within the community.

There are parallels here with the cycle of four quadrants we outlined earlier. But what Lave and Wenger add is a stronger emphasis on the social nature of learning and, perhaps most importantly, an idea of knowledge being located and created in a community of practice in which you can position yourself. It is the idea of *positionality* that we will now pursue in order to get to grips with how student teachers might be inducted into an understanding of teaching while working in classrooms.

As we have already indicated, the students we tracked through their training in school were eager to position themselves as full participants in the community of practice that is teaching. The fact that they were expected to teach, if only small groups, and were given ideas for tasks which were to be implemented in school confirmed their need to perceive themselves as full participants. Yet our analyses of their conversations with their mentors and our observations of them on task unsurprisingly revealed that they were often far from demonstrating competence and informed understanding in the way that they implemented the tasks. Their attempts at full participation would appear to be premature.

An enhancement of student learning and performance would have been easier for the mentors to manage in mentoring conversations had the students perceived themselves as learners in the classrooms. However, as we have already indicated, they saw themselves as polite guests and hence fellow teachers who were being given access to somewhere where they could teach. Mentors were often blocked by students when they attempted to offer unrequested advice on task-setting. Similarly students rarely gave mentors easy opportunities to evaluate student actions. Students appeared to present themselves as effective operators in classrooms and did not want to be seen as anything else. Yet students revealed in interviews that they wanted constructive criticism from their mentors. The management of criticism is an important part of mentoring and will be tackled in Chapter 3.

We suggest that part of the reason for student ambiguity over criticism is that there was no opportunity in the classrooms we observed for the students to act in the way that Lave and Wenger describe as peripheral participation. In other words, they did not position themselves on the edge of the action but attempted to act as full participants. They did not, unsurprisingly, always operate very well as teachers, but because they had positioned themselves as full and not peripheral participants it was not easy for their mentors to explore with them what might have led to a more competent performance.

We suggest that Lave and Wenger's idea of *legitimate peripheral participation* is a useful one for mentors to keep in mind when students are learning in their classrooms. Primary school classrooms are busy places where extra pairs of hands are always welcomed and well used. The classrooms have a strong activity focus and doing nothing is regarded as akin to idleness. Yet there seems to be a strong case to be made for resisting students' impatience and for refusing to accept every offer of help they make. The case rests on the need to regard them as learners who have slowly to acquire a complex understanding of a set of intricate and creative processes. Teaching is not easy and learning to teach is even more difficult.

One way of managing peripheral participation and of legitimating it is to emphasize student observation skills and the insights into the individual learning and behaviour patterns of children that these can produce. In order to legitimate these activities in the eyes of the students, mentors need to take student observations seriously and provide time to discuss them with students in ways that relate student observations to those that they have made themselves. Observations are usually better for a focus.

At this point we can return to a suggestion we made when discussing student progression through the quadrants we outlined earlier in this chapter and the importance of mentoring conversations in managing that progression. We proposed then that one way of directing student learning was by finding focuses for student learning that might not always involve them in teaching. This approach would involve mentors in identifying, with students, what elements of their own learning and what aspects of classroom life they were to take as a focus. Such an approach would make a headlong dive into the complexities of classroom dynamics an impossibility and would legitimate the students' right to deal with only small segments of the activities that make up classroom life. In other words, students' peripheral participation as learners would be legitimated.

## Is active mentoring the same as teaching?

Mentoring is perhaps a strange word to describe what we are advocating. Twentieth-century mentoring in the world of business, for example, is often simply a question of showing the ropes to a newcomer and is based on the assumption that the new member of staff may not know how a particular company operates but will have the basic qualifications demanded by the job. In this case the induction is into the subtleties and nuances of the meaning systems that are the features of a particular workplace. Induction will rarely involve the mentor in actual training and make few, if any, demands on the mentor as teacher of the newcomer.

Mentoring in initial teacher training is very different as it does involve mentors in teaching students. Margaret Wilkin reminds us that we need to think of mentoring as an active process (1995). In other words, to mentor is to teach. Well, you might say, if teachers can't mentor in a teacherly way, who can? Certainly teachers have a wealth of understanding about how to guide and support learning on which they can draw. Nevertheless active mentoring is not simply a question of transferring skills used with children and applying them to students.

Let us consider some of the skills involved in active mentoring. You may wish to add more of your own to the list. Ours is as follows:

- listening to students;
- modelling teaching and general classroom management;

- analysing and discussing one's own practice;
- observing students;
- negotiating with students their own learning goals;
- supporting students as they teach;
- encouraging focused observations of classroom events;
- encouraging focused student self-assessments;
- providing constructive criticism for students;
- highlighting what students can learn from an analysis of practice.

All of these depend on students being allowed to be seen as learners in classrooms.

Some features from the list, for example modelling practice, will be more important early in a student's training programme when the scaffolding or structured support of student learning has to be more finely focused. What then do we mean by scaffolding? In its strictest sense it is the provision of rapidly responsive support that enables a learner to achieve a learning goal. In primary classrooms we can see teachers scaffolding the learning of pupils in a variety of ways. These might include clear goal-setting to enable pupils to select only what is relevant in a task. It frequently involves quite precise resourcing of tasks to limit the way a pupil might attack a task. A common example, which we shall return to in Chapter 7, is to ban Sellotape in construction activities. Scaffolding also often involves teachers in the careful monitoring of pupils while they are on task so that quick and appropriate interventions, such as providing the appropriate language, can be made by teachers in order to assist the learning of pupils.

When we consider how mentors might scaffold the learning of students we can see that the first two examples of scaffolding in the previous paragraph (goal setting and resourcing) can be carried out in relative privacy. The final example (intervention) is more public and can, therefore, make aspects of scaffolding quite a delicate mentor activity.

Students are frequently worried about what they regard as the undermining of their authority if the teacherly support of a mentor is too direct and too public. Much mentor scaffolding will therefore occur in discussions with students before and after teaching events. We pay particular attention to this aspect of mentoring in Chapter 3. At this point we would simply want to emphasize the importance of these conversations. They provide the main opportunities for negotiating student learning goals around the tasks that they are planning for pupils. In Chapter 3 we shall look at how tasks may be negotiated between mentors and students. In Chapter 7 we look at task negotiation in more detail in a different context when we draw on the work of Doyle (1986) to examine how teachers and pupils negotiate the level of demand presented by an activity from which pupils are intended to learn.

There are, however, times when active mentoring while the student is teaching is also a useful way of scaffolding student learning. One way of licensing interventions while a student is teaching is to make team-teaching a common occurrence. We discuss this in Chapter 4. At this point we simply indicate that team-teaching is another way of legitimating the peripheral participation of students in the activities that comprise teaching.

## Is mentoring the same as counselling?

So far we have concentrated on mentoring as a way of bringing students into an understanding of the skills of teaching. We have almost implied that students' own feelings get in the way of the work of mentors as they attempt to enlighten students. We have pointed out that students enter their training wanting to *be* teachers and not simply to learn how to teach. We have suggested that this goal can inhibit student learning. However students are right to want to emphasize the importance of being a teacher. Developing a sense of oneself as a teacher is an important aspect of being effective at and enjoying teaching. This aspect of the development of student teachers can present particular challenges for mentors. We shall discuss but a few of them.

The biggest problem may occur if there is a dramatic mismatch between the picture a mentor holds of a good teacher and that held dear by the student she or he has been allocated. As we have already indicated students frequently want to cling to the images of being a teacher that have motivated them into teacher training. One way out of a major mismatch may be to arrange a reallocation to achieve a better match. However, if this were to happen, the student would arguably be acquiring a relatively narrow training in which she or he was not being encouraged to question assumptions or explore other possibilities for practice. Although students often find mismatch uncomfortable it can be managed by mentors who recognize it, name it and work with it quite openly. Mentors may not change students' images of how they want to operate, and perhaps should not even try, but they can perhaps enable students to explore the implications of wider varieties of practice.

Other challenges may be less dramatic and perhaps more common. Being a teacher is clearly more than putting into practice a set of skills. It is also a question of acting out one's value system on a daily basis. It demands that one puts oneself on the line, often in quite contentious situations. It is risky and can be soul-destroying when things go wrong. Learning to teach in the public arena of a classroom is particularly risky and therefore extremely stressful. Consequently there is a counselling element to mentoring. There is a need to attend to the whole student.

This aspect of a mentor's role can perhaps be separated from the teacherly mentor role through, for example, the use of what is sometimes called circle time in primary school practice (Mosley, 1991). In circle time sessions, ground-rules of confidentiality are agreed and fears and triumphs can be shared by students in an open climate. Where we have seen this in operation, 30 minutes have been set aside at the end of each week and the sessions have been run by the senior mentor in the school for all the students placed there.

Students' emotional responses to learning to teach have to be taken seriously. If they are not, there is the strong likelihood that unhappy students will either not stay the course or do so ineffectively and become unhappy teachers. However we have been arguing strongly throughout this chapter that mentoring is a complex teaching role. Consequently we see mentor-as-counsellor as an important aspect of that role but not the major one.

## Being a mentor

We have talked at length about student learning. We have particularly emphasized the work of Jean Lave and her perspective on teaching as a community of practice in which all participants are learning and at the same time shaping the understandings that operate within the community. We hope that you will use this text in ways that recognize your contributions as learners and participants in shaping understandings of mentoring. In the chapters that follow we shall be drawing on information we have gathered in primary schools as mentors worked with student teachers. We offer them to you as vehicles for stimulating your own thinking about your own practices in school. We expect that some of what we have found will differ from your experiences. None the less we hope that the ideas that we put forward will help you as you define and test your views of what makes a good mentor.

## Further reading

We cannot do justice to the carefully argued work of Lave and her associates in the summary we have provided. A good introduction is, Lave, J. (1993) The practice of learning, in S. Chaiklin and J. Lave (eds) *Understanding Practice: Perspectives on Activity and Context*, Cambridge, CUP. Other excellent collections of papers on situated cognition are Resnick, L., Levine, J. and Teasley, S. (eds) (1993) *Socially Shared Cognition*, Washington, APA, and Wertsch, J., Del Rio, P. and Alvarez, A. (eds) (1995) *Sociocultural Studies of Mind*, Cambridge, CUP.

James Calderhead has written extensively on the development of beginning teachers and the preconceptions they bring with them. See for example Calderhead, J. (1988) The development of knowledge structures in learning to teach, in J. Calderhead (ed.) *Teachers' Professional Learning*, London, Falmer.

John, P. (1995a) Understanding the apprenticeship of observation in initial teacher education: exploring student teachers' implicit theories of teaching and learning, in G. Claxton, T. Atkinson, M. Osborn and M. Wallace (eds) *Liberating the Learner: Lessons for Professional Development in Education*, London, Routledge is a detailed study of the preconceptions that student teachers bring to their training.

A useful collection of papers on student learning is Harvard, G. and Hodkinson, P. (eds) (1994) *Action and Reflection in Teacher Education*, Norwood, Ablex. The collection covers, among other topics, reflective practice (Zeichner); acquisition of theory (Eraut); accessing practical classroom knowledge (Brown); and competences (the editors).

Though addressed to a secondary teaching audience the next book is worth examining for its detailed coverage of the relationships between current understandings of, for example, intelligent skill development, professional thinking and learning and the practice of mentoring. Tomlinson, P. (1995) *Understanding Mentoring*, Buckingham, Open University Press.

# SECTION II

# MENTORING

# CONVERSATIONS

## What is a mentoring conversation?

When is a conversation between a mentor and a student a mentoring conversation? Is a snatched discussion about resources while walking towards
the classroom a mentoring conversation? Is the kind of rapid reaction
response made while teaching alongside a student a mentoring conversation? Is a chat about who is who in the school, as a student is given a lift
to school, a mentoring conversation? We would argue that all of these conversations are an important part of mentoring, as it is often through conversations of this kind that students are inducted into ways of seeing and
acting that are part of professional practice in a school.

In this chapter, however, we shall be considering only one type of conversation. We shall be looking at what goes on between mentors and students in the conversations that take place before teaching sessions in order
to plan the sessions or soon after teaching has taken place in order to evaluate what has occurred. We shall examine the conversations that take place
while teaching together in Chapter 4 and we shall tackle seminars in Chapter
5.

Most training programmes see the planning and evaluation conversations
between teacher-mentors and students to be at the heart of mentor–
student relationships. We shall, however, be suggesting that although these
conversations are important they cannot be used to cover all aspects of the
students' teacher training curriculum. They are, we shall argue, limited by
the fact that they are so often tightly connected to the implementation of

classroom tasks for pupils. Wide-ranging discussion of general principles of teaching and learning, for example, may be easier to manage in seminar sessions which are slightly distanced from the immediate needs of children in classrooms. Mentoring conversations which focus on task implementation can often perhaps do no more than highlight aspects of student learning. In Chapter 7 we indicate some of the aspects of practice that can be highlighted in these conversations.

Managing the conversations that occur around the focus of setting tasks for pupils in ways that enable students to learn from them is a major challenge for mentors. We suggest that it demands a double-level use of the conversations about tasks for children. Firstly the conversations need to focus on pupil learning and secondly, and simultaneously, they need to attend to the learning needs of students. Managing all of this in polite conversations which are treating the students as 'almost colleagues' is not easy.

The difficulty is demonstrated by the valiant attempts of the mentor in the following extract to shift a student to a situation where the student might learn from what the mentor had to offer. TM is the teacher-mentor and ST the student teacher. The subject area was religious and moral education, the children were in Year 1 and the task under discussion was making a welcome card for a new member of the class.

*TM (to ST):* What about you, how did yours go?
*ST:* Very well, but D was a bit silly. The others did really well, I was surprised.
*TM:* Yes they did, didn't they?
*ST:* We did talk a lot about colours, whether they made them feel angry or happy, and then we mixed colours to match the colours of their uniform.
*TM:* So you were pleased with it. Would you do it again?
*ST:* Yes but not with D.
*TM:* So how would you adapt it for him?
*ST:* Well I think he should be brought in more slowly. I think that he just needed to have the experience of mixing colours.
*TM:* Yes, so how would you adapt your activity? I mean next time, if for instance you have got children who have not got painting experience, how would you have dealt with it?
*ST:* Well I think I would have given them the paints and just let them have a session mixing paints.
*TM:* I am just thinking about your religious and moral education task though, because you are coming down on the art side. Thinking about the religious and moral education, how could you have done that activity another way? Perhaps basing it on a different medium?
*ST:* Well, we had done colouring before. I wanted to do something different.

*TM:* Yes but you needed to keep sight of your religious and moral education objectives. But of course the thing to remember is that if
you have got someone who is not perhaps as capable in a group
they are picking up a lot from other children.

In our discussions of mentoring conversations we shall be drawing heavily on information we gathered as a result of being able to tape-record mentors and students while they talked together before or after periods when
the students were teaching. We shall particularly use data from a finely
detailed analysis of the talk that was recorded over one year of the study.
The remaining taped conversations gathered over the subsequent two years
of the study are used only to provide illustrative examples. We call on these
quite extensively later in the chapter when we look at how mentors developed student understandings of practice through conversations about activities in classrooms.

We asked mentors and students to tape-record their conversations in
order to find out what went on when mentors and students had time to
talk. We wanted to get a feel for what mentors offered students and what
students wanted from their mentors. As the conversations raise a number
of issues, we shall start by giving an overview of what we found as a result
of our detailed analysis of conversations over one year of the programme.

## What did the mentors talk about?

We looked separately at the talk of mentors and students in order to discover the actual content of the talk of each participant. Mentors' talk was
mainly geared to assisting students as they planned tasks prior to teaching
sessions. The conversations lasted between five and 20 minutes and the
data we shall discuss were based on five hours of talk between 11 mentors and 21 students. The data analysis process is given in Collison and
Edwards (1994) and in Edwards and Collison (1995a).

A form of data-driven content analysis (Edwards and Talbot, 1994) was
used. This method of data analysis allowed us to organize the information
so that the talk could be sorted in categories that indicated what was being
discussed. When we analysed what the mentors talked about we found, to
the nearest whole number, that 34 per cent of mentor talk focused on the
resourcing of tasks: these were largely statements on how to set out classroom materials. Twenty-six per cent of talk was related to the students'
own progress. Much of this was related to finding out what students needed to be doing in school in order to meet their own curriculum needs.
Seven per cent of talk provided specific information about children and was
in direct response to students' questions as they constructed profiles of children. Discipline and values were evident implicitly in talk but were not made
explicit in statements about general principles. Talk of this kind accounted
for 3 per cent of what the mentors said. Talk related to teaching as the

management of pupil learning and the curriculum was 8 per cent of talk. Twenty-two per cent of talk was not classified as it was, for example, short statements of clarification such as 'Yes she is James's mum'.

Mentor talk seemed to focus particularly on two areas: firstly on the students' successful task-setting and secondly on what the students needed to do in order to meet the demands of their own higher education curriculum. There was little evidence of mentors encouraging students to think critically about their own actions (the majority of talk that encouraged student reflection on their practice came from one mentor) or of mentors challenging student preconceptions. The mentors were, however, offering the students safe places for their trial and error learning and attended to students' needs by identifying learning situations for future sessions at the school. Matters of values, discipline and pupil learning all received relatively little attention. Quite clearly these conversations were not acting as situations in which students were being encouraged to learn general principles from an examination of particular events.

We would argue that it was too much to expect that discussions which focused on task-setting for pupils should also be opportunities for a consideration of what the mentors themselves described as 'theory'. When mentors and students worked together to plan pupil tasks, the expert teachers who were the mentors appeared to be calling upon Shulman's amalgam of knowledge about what is to be taught and knowledge about pedagogy or teaching and learning (Shulman, 1987). Shulman, as we pointed out in Chapter 2, identifies this kind of knowledge as 'the unique province of teachers'.

His use of the word *amalgam* is an interesting one as once an amalgam is made it is difficult to re-create the constituent parts. We found, for example, that several of the mentors who allowed themselves to be recorded tried to connect practical advice to general psychological principles but appeared to find it extremely difficult to do so (Edwards and Collison, 1995a). They were attempting to meet what they saw to be student need and to take the task-setting exercise beyond the 'here and now'. They tried to provide the students with more general frameworks for decision making about tasks, but were unwilling or unable at that moment to call up the precise language which would have allowed them to communicate the points that they wanted to make. It is difficult, for example, to make much of the following statement, which was the result of a mentor seeing, quite rightly, the need to go beyond the here and now in order to assist the learning of the students.

> So again with these opposites, they reinforce each idea, so if you get one that has worked and one that hasn't . . .

Arguably the ability to call up what many mentors in interviews labelled as 'theory' is not what is required. However the ability to identify and highlight the general principles underlying successful practice might be. But even that is not easy.

One of the problems faced by expert teachers who become teachers of their teaching expertise is how difficult it is to make their tacit professional knowledge explicit and readily available in ways that a novice can grasp or even recognize. When we attempt to tackle this problem in Chapter 9 we shall be examining the use of dilemmas or puzzles in teaching as a way of helping the tacit knowledge of mentors become more explicitly available to students. There we shall be suggesting that joint exploration by mentors and students of dilemmas or problematic areas in practice provide an opportunity for sharing understandings.

However the joint analysis of teaching dilemmas, for example how to encourage problem-solving talk in group work, is challenging. It may be an activity that should be restricted only to the most competent of students. It does not therefore solve the problem of how to pass on principles of practice when students perhaps need most help. Arguably, it is in the early stages of a student's learning to teach that mentors are likely to want to provide the most explicit support, and therefore may need to communicate quite precise and detailed principles. It is also likely that the students who most need explicit advice are those who remain most oblivious when it is offered in a conversational tone.

Our evidence seems to suggest that the immediacy of classrooms, and of the needs of pupils in them, mean that discussions about the implementation of tasks for pupils limit the usefulness of mentoring conversations for students' wider understandings of general principles. We shall return to this topic in Chapter 5.

## What did the students talk about?

We divided student talk into two areas: planning and evaluation-related talk. Sixty-two per cent of their talk was concerned with planning and 26 per cent with evaluation. (Twelve per cent was not classified.) Not surprisingly the analysis of student contributions to the conversations revealed similar concerns to those evident in the mentors' talk. (The figures are to the nearest whole numbers; see Edwards, in press.)

Forty-eight per cent of talk was related to planning the implementation of tasks. Eight per cent focused on their own curricular needs, 3 per cent of talk related planning to children's learning, in relation to task implementation, and 2 per cent of talk was questions about the schools' longer-term curriculum planning. Eight per cent of their talk was comments on their own performance, 5 per cent was related to task evaluation and suggestions for the modification of tasks they had implemented. Ten per cent of talk drew on observations of children working with tasks in relation to the design of the tasks. Observations of children on task which were related to pupil learning accounted for 2 per cent of talk and comments on teacher performance were even fewer at 0.1 per cent of student talk. Evidence of their having grasped anything new in the conversations was of course difficult to discern; however, a search for students' recognition of any general insights gained revealed that overt evidence of learning was evident in 1 per cent of the talk.

When we went further than a simple analysis of *what* the students talked about and examined *how* they spoke to their mentors we entered some interesting territory. We looked at how the students presented themselves to mentors and from that we hypothesized about what the students expect-ed the mentors to want from them (Edwards, in press). We played with the idea of 'addressivity' which is used in literary criticism by followers of the work of Bakhtin (see for example Morris, 1994). This allowed us to see the style of interaction that students were using when talking to their mentors as a key to how they perceived their relationships with their mentors. According to Bakhtin, speakers select genres or styles of presentation which meet what they believe to meet the expectations of the listener. Examples of styles currently available to speakers in the UK include, for example, parent/child, employer/employee and friend/friend. Examination of the selection of a particular style can, as a result, reveal a great deal about how a speaker is positioning him or herself in the relationship that is represented by the conversation.

This form of analysis revealed that students were frequently selecting a particular style of interaction with their mentors and were using it as they negotiated the insertion of the tasks they had prepared for pupils into the well-established rhythms of the classrooms in which they were placed. The style was that of polite guest/host. The language and mode of inter-action of polite guest is evident in, for example the following set of student statements.

> Well actually I, well we've both had an idea haven't we? / A torch or something with different colours of cellophane and see what colours they make when we put more colours with it.

> Another tack we could take, if you like, would be, can I do silhou-ettes and working in pairs and drawing each others' silhouettes?

In each example the student had an idea about a task but was offering it in a style that was couched in tentativeness. The following are also exam-ples of a tentative offering of expertise.

> I did a bit of work on that over the summer . . .

> My youngest one is on to Fuzz Buzz at the moment [in his school] . . .

On the other hand, when students responded to an invitation from a men-tor to disclose what had been planned for the next session, there was no tentativeness. The tentative mode of offering what were in effect 'tasks as gifts' seemed to be serving a specific purpose in situations where students were uncertain of their right of entry into the dynamics of an established classroom. It asserted the positions of the students as legitimate teachers and placed the mentors as hosts in a position where it was difficult to refuse the gifts however unsatisfactory they might be. All the mentors could do with unsatisfactory gifts was to endeavour to ensure that they did not disrupt the pupils.

The idea of the selection of style of interaction is helpful, not only because it allows us to consider the style students selected, but also because it raises questions about those styles that were not chosen. Interestingly, in the conversations we analysed, a style of 'student as learner/mentor as teacher of student' was not evident.

The idea of mentor as host is certainly plausible when we remember that the mentors saw their primary purpose to be to provide safe places for student trial and error learning. In addition the idea of tasks as entry gifts gains support when we examine how the gifts were inserted into the rhythm and balance of the classroom. Both students and mentors wanted the tasks to be implemented successfully. This aim is evident in the amount of talk by both the mentors and the students on the topic of task implementation. The students were presenting themselves to their mentors as operators and not as learners. Their position as actors and not as learners was legitimated by the success of the tasks they brought as gifts.

It was important that the tasks were successful. We have suggested elsewhere (Collison and Edwards, 1994) that mentors and students were acting together in ways that allowed the students to reduce the riskiness of the tasks they were designing and were, as a consequence, limiting the opportunities for learning available for the students. In that argument we drew on the work of Walter Doyle (1986).

His work on how teachers and pupils negotiate tasks in classrooms is helpful. His analysis of the processes of negotiation between teachers and pupils in classrooms suggests that the reduction of risk of failure at a task is attractive to both the teachers and the learners. A simple routine classroom task is more likely to be completed successfully with minimal pupil disruption. Consequently, argues Doyle, teachers collude with pupils who want easy tasks by providing so much scaffolding for tasks that pupils do little more than follow instructions. One side effect is that low-risk tasks can limit the challenge that can lead to pupil learning (see Chapter 7).

When we apply Doyle's ideas to teacher education and look at the learning of student teachers we can begin to see similar forces at work. The religious and moral education task evaluation we discussed earlier in the chapter is an example of how students attempt to reduce the challenge of the tasks they set for children and hence for themselves. Neither mentors nor students want student tasks to fail. Mentors don't want pupil disruption and they want to sustain student confidence. Students, as we have already argued, don't want public failure. However, reducing the risk elements in the tasks that students set in classrooms makes the task of task implementation less of a challenge and, we suggest, less of a learning opportunity for students.

There was evidence throughout the mentor–student conversations of students keeping the discussion at the level of practical detail that provided careful scaffolding for them as they planned the implementation of tasks. Some students clearly resisted attempts on the part of some mentors to complicate the processes of task implementation and to make it more of a risky activity. The following extract from a conversation between a teacher-mentor (TM) and two student teachers (ST1 and ST2) illustrates how students can avoid elements of uncertainty in practice. The discussion is about Christmas cards.

*TM:* Do you want to do the tub at the bottom a different colour?
*ST1:* We could do a few different colour ones, couldn't we? Just cut some card out of something.
*ST2:* But we will need to find some card if we can't use the blue.
*ST1:* We need to keep it simple, don't we?
*TM:* That is why I was suggesting a template . . .

Here the students appear almost to be dominating the conversation. They begin to dismiss the mentor's idea to the extent that he feels the need to reassert his authority. It would seem that the students perceived the mentor's role to be to facilitate but not to complicate the insertion of tasks into the classroom. At the same time the position of mentors as gatekeepers to the classrooms had to be acknowledged.

Our analysis paints a rather conservative picture of the purpose of mentor–student talk about tasks. This interpretation is given weight by other evidence we gathered in interviews and questionnaires over three years. These findings revealed that the mentors in the study wanted the students they mentored to be people who fitted into their classrooms and their schools. At the same time they valued the new ideas that the students brought with them. The students were, as a result, faced with a paradox. They need to bring fresh ideas yet were required to implement them in non-disruptive ways. The polite-guest perspective on the way that students interacted with mentors seems to relate to what the mentors were themselves saying about their expectations of students.

The polite-guest style of interaction and the emphasis on successful task implementation seemed to have some advantages. It at least enabled the students to manage the paradox of mentor expectations we have just outlined. None the less, both the type of interaction and the focus on the ease of task implementation created some important gaps in the content of the conversation that perhaps needed either to be addressed elsewhere in the student experience or to be brought explicitly into interactions about task. There was, for example, little attention paid to pupil learning in the conversations we analysed. No references were made to pupils' emotional state or motivation. In addition there was little evidence of students attempting to learn explicitly from watching teacher actions in the classroom.

## What are students learning in conversations about tasks?

This is a difficult question to answer. We might be able to tell whether they are learning, for example, how to implement tasks, or how to manage a class in the potentially chaotic five minutes before dinner, by looking at how well they do that before and after advice from their mentors. However we cannot easily assess the incidental learning, for example about relations with parents, that might be occurring when mentors are helping students to plan and evaluate. Furthermore, we have no way of demonstrating how that incidental learning is played out in practice.

In addition we are well aware that we are offering you evidence from a small-scale study of one programme, and repeat that this evidence is given as a starting point for your own speculations about mentor practice. But let us nonetheless consider some of the implications of the findings we have so far presented.

The emphasis that was placed in the conversations on successful task implementation in the public arena of classrooms appears to have considerable limitations. Firstly the focus on immediate success means that students were not seeking, or receiving, general learning principles from their mentors. What they were getting was advice on how to manage the resources that were available to them in order to create activities for pupils. Advice on using resources may, however, simply represent what teaching in primary schools actually *is*. Huberman describes classroom teachers as instructional handymen.

> The classroom teacher remains essentially a 'tinkerer' or 'instructional handyman' who can pull together a host of materials lying around at various stages of a construction or repair job. These materials meet the particular need that emerges at a specific point and are fashioned to fit that particular purpose.
>
> (Huberman, 1995: 196)

If this is the case, maybe the mentors who were recorded as they talked to students were giving the students exactly what was needed.

In the same paper Huberman argues that the fashioning to fit that occurs does not rest on a codified body of knowledge but on a set of individual experiences and anticipations acquired over time while teaching. If Huberman is correct about the idiosyncratic nature of teaching, and most people writing on teacher knowledge would agree with him (see for example Clandenin and Connelly, 1986), then the teasing out of general principles from an examination of particular tasks requires a very high degree of mentor self-awareness and knowledge of one's own practice. The fact that a number of mentor training programmes start with the analysis of one's own practice as a teacher of children testifies to the importance of this ingredient in sound mentoring.

## Areas for development

### *Finding a focus for student learning*

Yet however self-aware one might be, it is difficult to respond to the vast range of learning points for students that might arise from the planning and evaluation of just one student-led task. In Chapter 2 we suggested that task-setting for pupils may also involve the mentor in setting limits to the tasks so that they are also used as vehicles for student learning. Doyle (1986) suggests that one way of reducing the risk in tasks, while maintaining the challenge, is to highlight what is important for pupil learning in them. Again we might apply Doyle's ideas to teacher training.

Our data indicate that if this suggestion is taken up the limiting process should start at the planning stage. In the student talk we have just discussed, evaluation talk was less frequent than talk related to planning. In addition the talk that was regarded as evaluatory provided little evidence that students had acquired the general principles that lie behind the management of pupil learning in classrooms.

In Chapter 5 we suggest that much might be gained from all the mentors in a school being aware of the students' curriculum and the part that seminar activities in schools might play in developing students' understanding of general principles. A coherently planned set of learning experiences for students demands that mentors direct student learning towards their own current curriculum goals as they work on tasks with children. This is where we return to the idea of using pupil tasks at two levels that we mentioned earlier in this chapter. The two levels of pupil learning and student learning might be brought together in a planning session by starting with the student learning need. The following outline of a planning conversation will give some flavour of what we mean.

1 Identify student learning focus: managing paired tasks.
2 Identify intended pupil learning outcomes. Discuss setting up weighing tasks.
3 Discuss use of student time: when to 'teach' and when to 'watch'.
4 Identify evaluation points: who, if anyone, dominates in the interaction; what is said (type of pupil language); pupil recording.

The evaluation conversation would then focus on the evidence gathered under the evaluation points that had been identified in the planning conversation.

## Theory and practice

In Chapter 7 we shall be examining a few of the principles of practice that frequently need to be tackled by mentors as they induct students into managing the learning of pupils. These topics include lesson planning and evaluation, group work, task analysis, the assessment of pupils and the use of teacher time. These topics are core elements in any teacher training programme and need to be incorporated into the learning experiences of students as they work in classrooms.

We found no evidence, in the conversations from the first year of the programme, of the use of classroom tasks at two levels, in which the topics we have just listed formed the second-level use of the tasks set for pupils. What seemed to be occurring in the data we collected, both in the conversations and in interviews and questionnaires, was in fact evidence of an extension of the theory–practice divide that beset teacher education in the UK until the early 1980s and was illustrated in Figure 2.1. Our evidence indicated that classrooms were being seen by mentors as places for trial and error actions and that although there was a need for 'theory', or a discussion of more general principles, the majority of the mentors felt it should be provided by higher education. From the mid-1980s until recently, the problem of the theory–practice divide was tackled by higher education departments of education through government funded strategies for ensuring that university staff received regular opportunities to update their teaching skills in schools. The funding has now been withdrawn.

There is some irony in the fact that school-based teaching appears to be creating a separation of theory and practice that the universities themselves endeavoured so hard to erode. We shall tackle the relationships between schools and universities in Chapter 11, and argue there that there is a place for theory and, specifically, for a partnership between schools and universities in the creation of educational theory which, in part, arises in practice and is tested and developed in practice.

## Mentors as critics of student practice

The data also seemed to indicate that the rights of the mentors were not clear. Hosts can be abused by their guests. We have already discussed how a determined student can resist what a mentor tries to offer. We also have evidence from other partnership arrangements of mentors' reluctance to criticize students' practice for fear of discouraging, and of unwillingness to correct even basic errors, for example in spelling and grammar on displays.

In the conversational data we subjected to fine analysis and have just discussed, we found no examples of mentors' corrections or criticism, though their non-occurrence could be a feature of the fact that we received only the conversations that were taped and passed to us. In Chapter 8 we shall be looking at the role of mentors in the assessment of students and simply suggest at this point that not only is mentoring about encouraging the students, but it may involve mentors in exercising their rights to point out where errors are occurring before they escalate.

However, by giving some attention to the role of the mentor as critic and judge we are identifying yet another weakness in a mentor–student relationship that focuses only on student performance in a classroom. The focus on student performance can limit mentor interactions with students to an encouragement and shaping of aspects of performance. We would argue that mentoring has to be more than a weak use of behaviourist or behaviour modification principles. Rather we are suggesting a view of mentoring which involves goal setting for student learning and which fits into the framework we gave in Figure 2.2. One result of negotiating a focus for student learning and of demanding student consideration of what they have learnt from task implementation, may be that mentoring becomes more easily the exploration and shaping of understandings of some principles of practice.

In the following extract, which comes from data collected later in the study, we can see how one mentor successfully offered constructive criticism to students in an evaluation conversation. You will note that she is not engaging in polite conversation. Rather she is highlighting with some clarity where improvements are needed. The students recognize what she is doing and clearly value it. The teacher-mentor (TM) is talking to two students (STs).

*TM:* Art this afternoon, I like the idea of introducing a lot of vocabulary to do with the topic. Do you want the bad points first?

*ST1/ST2:* Yes!

*TM:* I think that now you know the children better that we should be building in a lot more differentiation into a class art lesson like that. So that you focus on a skill but do it at different levels. Or develop different skills with different children.

*ST1:* So what would you have done? I mean how would you have done it?

*TM:* Well for some I would just do the colour matching, especially for B, thinking about how long he can concentrate for. Then for the brighter ones I might have said, 'This is mine, that's the basic shape, there's the mast. I want you to draw me three sails that are of different sizes. I want them graded, small, middle and large to fit on the mast.' Ways of making it problem-solving. But the activity is excellent. I don't want you feeling depressed by it.

*ST2:* No, that is what we need. We need you to tell us where to expand not only for the children but for us too. Just a suggestion. Would you perhaps one week demonstrate how you would get that across to the kids, how you would actually teach it?

*TM:* Sure.

### De-centring student performance

Seeing students as learners in classrooms returns us to the work of Lave and Wenger (1991) and Chaiklin and Lave (1993) which we outlined in Chapter 2. Their perspective on the induction of novices into the priorities and practices and the language in which these are expressed in a community of practice would suggest the need at times to de-centre the students' performance so that it is not always the main focus of formal mentoring conversations. If student success at task implementation were to be made less central, there would be the opportunity to structure conversations around, for example, student analysis of teacher performance.

Students don't find this easy. The following extract is from another conversation between the mentor and the two students whose conversation about differentiation in art sessions you have just read.

> *ST1:* It has been suggested that we sit in and observe you, not to take notes . . .
>
> *TM:* What about taking turns on Fridays, taking it in turns to observe? So one of you could observe first thing and hear some readers or hear your group read, sit in the reading corner and you can see what is going on.
>
> *ST2:* Yes you feel stupid actually just sitting there, you feel you should be doing something.
>
> *ST1:* And we have got to decide whether to look for anything specific or just general observations.

Both the mentor and the students in this extract were highly sensitive to the need to be doing something while in a classroom. Peripheral participation had to be disguised as a legitimate activity.

One way that we intervened as researchers in the programme we were examining was to suggest at the end of the first year of the programme that students should occasionally observe their mentors while the mentors were undertaking specific activities and discuss their observations. Those students who followed this advice reported with enthusiasm on the value of the activity for their own learning about practice. However, a few students resisted the suggestion and explained later that they did not regard it to be a legitimate use of their time in schools. The legitimating of what Lave and Wenger (1991) describe as peripheral participation in a community of practice would seem to be a useful step. One way of achieving its legitimating may be to create time for formal mentoring conversations that focus on topics other than the task implementation of students.

## What are the ingredients of an effective mentoring conversation?

The proof of the pudding is in the eating. Consequently an effective mentoring conversation, given our concern with student learning, is one in which students begin to develop their understandings of practice and learn something that can be seen to impact on their practice. Assessing the impact of a conversation is difficult. Yet it is possible to tease out, in our data gathered over the three years of the programme, how mentor advice has influenced student performance in, for example, how a task is introduced to a group of children. It is more difficult to trace the relationship between a developing understanding of general issues of practice and the advice that mentors provide. However it could be seen later in the programme in the way, for example, that students dealt with the unpredictability of a misbehaving child after a discussion of their concerns about classroom discipline.

Moving conversations with students away from simply the implementation of tasks to more general issues of practice is not always easy. As we have already demonstrated, students are quite capable of leading the conversation in the directions they want to take. And why not? We are discussing conversations and not lectures. But students do have considerable general concerns when they start to teach. Their greatest worry initially is usually the management of the pupils. The design of most teacher training programmes recognizes this. Yet we found very little evidence, in the taped conversations, of students discussing discipline and their concerns about this aspect of teaching. We suspect that this gap was due in part to the curriculum task focus of the conversations that were recorded and in part to the students' reluctance to reveal their anxieties to their mentors. They did however talk to their fellow students about discipline worries.

There were, none the less, some mentors who were able to create conversational climates that enabled students to disclose their concerns. This disclosure provided valuable opportunities for the mentors to move the conversation away from task implementation to more general task management and discipline issues. In the following extract from one of the conversations which occurred later in the programme and was not analysed in detail, the mentor (TM) has just completed a long description of how she organizes her reception class and herself as a resource within it. The student teachers (STs) have been listening with interest.

ST: What do you do when you've got, like, children on doing other activities and as you say you've got three or four or whatever, and they start getting up and wandering around and saying that they are bored doing that but there is no room in anywhere else?

TM: I don't often get that, but . . .

ST: I had noticed that they just wander around and . . . well can I go in there? And they keep coming to me . . .

TM: Well, the answer is no. The answer should be no. How many people are there over there? Well, if there are too many, then no, you can't. They're coming to you because they think that you might let them go somewhere where they are not allowed to go.

(ST: Yeah.) And if they know that you are going to say, how many people are over there? Three. Well how many should there be? Three. So you can't then, can you? Or if there are two say, how many are there? Two. How many are allowed? Three. OK, you can . . . what are you asking me for? You've got to make them independent. But you are not going to make them independent if you look at them and say . . .

ST:    (interrupts) . . . They ask Tim and they ask me, they're playing us off . . .

There may seem little exceptional to you in the conversation we have just provided. But it was in fact relatively rare for students to ask mentors the kind of general discipline-related question that opened the extract.

Certain mentors managed to achieve the conversational climate that encouraged students to raise more general questions and reveal their anxieties. These mentors were good listeners, and took seriously students' concerns. They demonstrated their listening by giving clearly focused responses that started from the students' perspectives. They gave useful answers that could easily be tried out by the students and they followed up a student's demonstration of a recommended strategy with praise in a later session. They were oriented to the students as learners and were operating as active mentors in all their interactions with students. The mentor who featured in the extract we have just discussed is the mentor whose style of interaction with students opens our discussion of active mentoring in the next chapter.

## Activities

1 Tape yourself in a conversation with a student or pair of students. You will, of course, require their permission. Listen to the tape and consider any of the following questions.

- Is the conversation mainly planning or mainly evaluation in focus?
- Do you mainly give advice or mainly ask questions?
- What kinds of questions do you ask? Do they elicit students' ideas about practice?
- How do you manage constructive criticism?
- Do the students ask your advice on teaching during the conversation?
- What topics, in addition to task implementation, do you touch on?

Using the list of questions, identify an aspect of the conversation which you think might benefit from a change in the way you tackled it. Identify strategies for the development of that aspect in future conversations with students. Tape-record a second conversation and assess your success. You could then use the evidence of your second conversation as a starting point for a discussion with colleagues (see Chapter 9).

2 Plan a planning conversation with a student using the outline we have provided in this chapter. Tape-record the planning conversation and the later evaluation discussion, with the agreement of the student. Examine the extent to which you were able to maintain the two levels of conversation we have been advocating, i.e. attention to the learning needs of both pupils and student. If possible discuss your findings with colleagues.

You may also wish to discuss the recordings from either of these activities with the students concerned.

## Further reading

We have not drawn on the important work of Donald Schön in our discussion of mentoring conversations. In fact we have made very little reference at all to 'reflection'. This is in part due to the fact that we believe that the use of reflection on practice in initial teacher education has recently suffered from an over-simplification: we prefer the idea of thinking about an event. It is also because we don't always find Schön's use for example of architecture and music particularly useful when considering preparation for action in unpredictable primary school classrooms. As Eraut (1995) notes, Schön's books 'contain no descriptions of such front-stage action in crowded environments'. Nevertheless Schön has been so influential that he should be read. The reading could then be followed by the two analyses of his work that we also list.

Schön, D. A. (1987) *Educating The Reflective Practitioner*, San Francisco, Jossey-Bass.

Gilroy, P. (1993) Reflections on Schön: an epistemological critique and a practical alternative, in P. Gilroy and M. Smith (eds) *International Analyses of Teacher Education*, Abingdon, Carfax.

Eraut, M. (1995) Schön shock: a case for reframing reflection-in-action? *Teachers and Teaching: theory and practice*, 1(1): 9–22.

A detailed examination of what can go wrong in mentoring conversations can be found in John, P. (1995b) The supervisory process in teacher education, in G. Claxton, T. Atkinson, M. Osborn and M. Wallace (eds) *Liberating the Learner*, London, Routledge.

# MENTORING IN

# ACTION IN

# CLASSROOMS

## Active mentoring while students teach

If teaching were a simple task student teachers could be shown how to do it and then left to master it through trial and improvement, but it is not. Teaching, as we have argued, is an extremely complex activity. In addition, too much student error can damage pupils. Effective teaching as displayed by an expert practitioner can, however, appear deceptively simple to a novice with little understanding of the scene being observed and the historical and future significance of events within it. There are many facets to the role of mentor, but if we acknowledge that one of them is to develop student teachers' understanding of children and classrooms, we cannot ignore the management of student learning in classrooms through active mentoring as students teach.

The mentoring conversations we discussed in the last chapter are an extremely important part of mentorship, but they are rarely responsive to students' immediate needs as they attempt to develop their own practices in action in classrooms. By definition, mentoring conversations related to planning and evaluation can only be *talking about* teaching. In order to learn about the activity of teaching, learning *how to see classrooms* and *how to respond to what one sees* while acting within them are also essential elements of learning as students move towards what Lave and Wenger (1991) describe as expert participation in the community of practice.

In Chapter 2 we talked about the difficulties involved in learning how to teach in the public arenas that are classrooms. In Chapter 3 we outlined the part that planning and evaluation mentoring conversations can play in giving direction and focus to student learning in classrooms. In this chapter we want to examine how mentors can shape student behaviour in ways that allow students to understand the dynamics of classroom life and their relationship to pupil learning. The particular challenge we shall trace in this chapter is how this is done without undermining the self-confidence of students as they operate publicly as managers of children's learning. As we emphasize throughout this book, one key to successful mentoring in initial teacher training is to see the students as learners.

If we return to the Vygotskian learning cycle we provided in Chapter 2, we can see that in quadrants B and C of Figure 2.2, not only is acting in classrooms a central activity, but it has to be managed in ways that enable students to learn from their activities. At the same time, a key feature of quadrant B and C experiences is that students learn to respond appropriately to the cues that are available in classrooms while they teach. In order to do this, students will at times require assistance from those whose lenses are better adapted to the nuances of classroom dynamics.

Knowing how best to respond to and assist the seeing of student teachers within a busy classroom is possibly the most intricate of mentor tasks. At the same time, working in classrooms also perhaps offers some of the best opportunities for guiding students' learning as they learn to exercise their developing *knowledge in action*. In this chapter we present case studies as starting points for the consideration of how to make the most of these opportunities for assisting the development of students while they are teaching. We provide three case studies of mentors as examples of relationships in which students appeared to be learning. In doing so we acknowledge that good mentoring practice is difficult to define and that, particularly, it will not be encapsulated in a set of procedures.

This chapter is different from those that preceded it. It contains a tentative theoretical account of what features might be required in interactive mentoring in classrooms. Set beside this tentative framing of 'mentoring while teaching' are a set of narrative accounts of mentoring in classrooms which are offered without commentary. These accounts are not the raw data from which we started our analyses of actions in classrooms, but draw on that data, and are presented as narratives to give some feel of the kinds of experiences that students were having.

The actual data were collected using a variation of the 'target child' method of continuous but focused observation first used by Sylva *et al.* (1980). The focuses of the observations were individual students as they worked with pupils. The observations allowed the recording of mentor actions when these involved the 'target students' (Edwards and Talbot, 1994). The target student observations were followed up by field notes written immediately after the observation had been completed. These allowed us to place the focused observations more firmly in the dynamics of a classroom.

A strength of the case studies is that there are substantial differences between the three mentors who are presented in them. Indeed, it is not our intention to suggest that these examples describe the only ways of mentoring effectively. Rather we intend to use the case studies to tease out themes that seem to represent aspects of effective practice.

## The case studies

The case study data come from observations of the classroom experiences of student teachers whilst on serial attachments to schools. As an element of the partnership arrangements in the programme we examined, student teachers were placed in pairs in classrooms on curriculum-centred school attachments which extended over an academic year. Cathy and Mark were mentors working with student teachers during the students' first year. Sue worked with student teachers in their second year of study.

Although the case studies reflect the different dispositions of the three mentors, there are some characteristics that they share. They all felt secure about their own classroom practices and did not appear to be disconcerted by the presence of 'would-be teachers' in their workspaces. They also shared a desire to continue their own professional development and tended to look on their work with students as one way of doing this. All three recognized that they were experts but they were interested in the ideas that the students brought with them from the university. Most importantly their attitude towards the student teachers was that the students are learners and that they may have as much need of teacher attention as do the pupils. All three recognized the importance of giving feedback and the value of spending time planning and evaluating lessons together with their student teachers. A strong element in their evaluations was student performance in relation to the complex processes of teaching.

We shall start by looking in quite general ways at each of the three mentors who exemplify active mentoring in the classroom. We shall at times refer to their behaviour as *contingent mentoring* because what they appear to be trying to do is to provide rapidly responsive scaffolded support for students in a variety of ways in response to student learning need. (We discuss scaffolding in pupil learning in some detail in Chapter 7.) After introducing the three teachers we shall draw on observations made of their practices to illustrate the techniques they used to support student learning in classrooms.

### Cathy

Cathy talks about her classroom as a workshop where students can try out new ideas. Her responsiveness to students' needs means that she is able to remove or replace scaffolding as required. Cathy keeps an eye on all that is happening in her class. Even when she has responsibility for the majority of the class she visits each student's group to talk with the children and, if relevant to the student's current needs, to model appropriate teacher actions. (Observation 1 presents an example of such a situation.)

Cathy encourages her students to experiment and sees her role partly as confidence-building so that students feel secure enough to try out new ideas. She wants, however, to prevent her students from making large mistakes, interpreting these as her error in wrongly judging the degree of support necessary. Thus she might intervene in a situation where a student teacher was close to losing control of the class. (See Observation 4.3.) Cathy believes that it is important to approach intervention in a way that does not destroy a student's authority. By modelling appropriate teacher behaviour she quietly structures support for students' actions. Her interventions come from a belief not that failures have to be avoided, but that students will learn more from assisted performance. If no immediate opportunity exists for Cathy to model appropriate teacher actions she will suggest that her students might like to observe her in a later teaching session. (See Observation 4.2.)

Cathy has a well-developed understanding of the students as learners and plans their progress. Observation 4.3 includes examples of how students manage the whole class in ways that Cathy has already highlighted for the two students concerned.

Cathy recognizes the value of feedback to student teachers. She uses her awareness of what has happened within the students' teaching to pick some successful aspect of the lesson as her opening remark and later brings the discussion to aspects that may have been less successful. Cathy rarely makes notes during the teaching session. This is partly because she is usually involved with teaching the rest of the class. But even when the opportunity arises she would not do so because she thinks that it is intimidating for the students. Cathy does provide her students with written feedback as appropriate but she completes 'crit' sheets after teaching sessions and not during them.

### Mark

A notable feature of Mark's approach to students placed in his classroom is the way that his actions appear to confirm the students as real teachers in the eyes of the children. This is clearly evident in Observation 4.4 when he waits for Alan, a student, to relinquish authority to him.

Mark sometimes suggests that his students should observe him or participate in a jointly planned lesson in a way that is almost orchestrated. During such a lesson he provides students with a running commentary, whenever possible explaining his actions and decisions. You could describe Mark's actions as providing a guided tour of his teaching.

Unlike Cathy, Mark's demonstration of teaching may not be directly in response to the students' current needs but may contribute to their wider understandings as beginning teachers. Observation 4.4 is an example of such a lesson. In this case the situation was used by Mark to illustrate the point that it is possible to know something but not know how to teach it. (This is an issue that we deal with in greater detail in Chapter 6.)

Mark believes that constructive criticism is very important and assists students as they evaluate. As can be seen in Observation 4.5, he is frequently to be found observing and writing notes that will inform subsequent discussions and form the basis of written feedback.

### Sue

A main plank of Sue's philosophy of education is that teaching is about promoting and maintaining learner self-esteem. She believes that it is only from a position of security that one can take risks to try out new and challenging tasks which can lead to development. An important feature of Sue's position is that she feels secure and unfazed by mistakes. She attributes this security to the atmosphere of her school where she is supported in her attempts to develop her own practice because she is allowed to make, and acknowledge, mistakes. Her attitude to mentoring in her classroom is that mistakes are part of the process of learning.

Whether her students are working with small groups of children or with the whole class, Sue manages to be involved with what is happening with them. Because mistakes are permissible, she is unlikely to intervene directly but she frequently talks briefly to them, helping them to understand classroom events as they occur. (See Observation 4.6.) She models teacher strategies through team-teaching but this is not the contingent shaping of context displayed by Cathy. Whilst Sue is more like Mark in this respect, she agrees with Cathy in feeling that it is too threatening to write notes whilst the student teachers are teaching.

It is important to stress that these case studies are not presented as perfect examples of mentorship. Indeed you may feel uncomfortable with aspects of the active mentoring we have just described. The observations of the practice of these three mentors do, however, allow us to explore some aspects of mentor action in classrooms. The list that follows indicates some of the features displayed by the three case study mentors. This list does not contain a complete description of an effective mentor; not least because the observations only cover aspects of mentoring that occur when actually teaching or as soon as possible after the event that is being discussed.

The active mentors we observed while they were working in classrooms:

- acknowledged student teachers as learners;
- promoted the confident practice of the students;
- were aware of the students' teaching, even when simultaneously responsible for the majority of the pupils;

- communicated with the students, however briefly, during teaching sessions in order to offer explanation or illumination of events as near as possible to the time they occurred;
- responded to the students' immediate needs for a model of appropriate teacher action;
- had some goals for student performance;
- were sensitive to students' need to be seen by the children as 'teachers';
- offered feedback, verbal and written, on the students' teaching.

Arguably we might be stretching an acceptable definition of *contingent* when we talk of contingent mentoring, because we include in our definition any relatively rapid response to students' perceived needs. Contingent mentoring, as we see it, appears to be a way of assisting student teachers towards more effective and hence more complete participation in the pedagogic activities of the classroom.

If you are a mentor you may want to consider your own practice and make additions to the behaviours we have listed. One behaviour that cannot feature in a list based on observations of actions in classrooms, but which one would want to include in any analysis of how mentors assist student performance, is the focusing of student actions as a result of careful prior planning and resourcing by the mentor.

In the observations that follow, four themes or types of active mentoring are demonstrated by the three mentors we have just described. The themes we have extracted are modelling, intervention, team-teaching and contingent dialogue.

## The themes

### Theme 1: Modelling

*Observation 4.1   Cathy with student teachers Rachel and Ann*

Setting: reception class

Rachel is working with six children testing the effect of gold and silver crayons on different-coloured paper. Ann has five children with her who are talking about and sorting autumn leaves. Cathy is working with a group of children on a writing task. She also has an eye on small groups of children who are constructing models with Mobilo or playing in the home corner. She glances occasionally at Rachel and Ann. Rachel is coping fairly well but Ann's group has drifted away from sorting the leaves into making collage faces with the leaves.

Cathy goes to Ann's group and suggests that they could sort the leaves into light and dark and spends a few minutes talking to the children about the leaves. She judges that two of the children have spent long enough at this activity and directs them to the free choice activities.

Cathy now visits Rachel's group. She talks to the children about their choices and encourages them to express reasons for their preferred combination of colours.

Cathy checks on Ann's group, discusses in which group to put a leaf that is dark on one side and light on the other.

Cathy returns to the writing table. Ann and Rachel continue with their groups. Ann is now using some of the questions that Cathy has just modelled. Cathy initiates tidying the classroom for break and requests that the light and dark leaves be kept so that she can show them to the whole class.

*Observation 4.2   Cathy with student teachers Rachel and Ann*

Setting: reception class

Cathy takes the register, then settles the class to listen to her as she explains the morning's activities. Rachel and Ann are observing. The two reception classes are holding a 'wedding' as part of their topic on people and work. The local vicar is coming in to explain about his work and to conduct a 'wedding' ceremony.

Cathy rehearses how she wants the children to greet Father John and sets very clear ground-rules for their behaviour. One rule is 'no calling out'. Stephen calls out an answer and is firmly ignored. Immediately he obeys the 'hand up' rule and Cathy chooses him to answer. In past weeks Rachel and Ann have both found Stephen's impulsiveness difficult to handle.

Cathy organizes the moving of chairs to another classroom (which is to be arranged for the 'wedding breakfast') and directs the children to go to the toilet on their way back. Ann and Rachel monitor the movement outside the classroom. The other reception class arrives and Cathy settles them ready for Father John.

### Theme 2: Intervention

*Observation 4.3   Cathy with student teachers Rachel and Ann*

Setting: reception class

During this time Cathy is listening to readers in the staff room. This arrangement has been planned in order to allow the students to have responsibility for the whole class. Rachel and Ann introduce 'time' by using a story to relate times of the day to routine activities and by showing a clock which is set at appropriate times. Ann introduces the task, which consists of colouring, cutting out and making a clock with moving hands, and allows the children to start the colouring element of the task.

Cathy returns to the classroom. Rachel asks Cathy for advice about how to handle Paul, one of the pupils with whom she has been having some difficulties. Cathy watches what is going on whilst she completes her reading records. Cathy reminds Rachel of the time (this is the third week that the students have been responsible for the timing of teaching sessions). Ann initiates clearing up, milk time, etc., and dismisses class.

Cathy then suggests to the students that they might like to consider strategies for managing the whole class. She reminds them how she always sets out the classroom ready for the arrival of the children. She tells the students that they are free to use whatever they like. She also reminds them of the need to move children from table to table. Cathy appears to be attempting to get the students to realize that it might be all right to have the whole class working on the same task whilst the children are colouring the clocks but that they won't be able to cope with the level of assistance the children will need to cut out and assemble their clocks.

After break Rachel begins her task for the day, which is to work with children as they print borders to make decorated notepaper for thank-you letters. She is working with three children at a time. Consequently Ann has responsibility for the remaining children, all of whom are working on the clock task.

Cathy speaks to Ann about the advisability of having so many children working on their clocks. Cathy helps by cutting out clock hands for some children and showing others (those she judges as able to do it themselves) what to do; Ann is not making any distinction between children.

Cathy asks Ann if it is 'all right if we work together?' Cathy removes one group from the clock-making task. She directs them to some construction blocks. Ann continues to cut out and fix clock hands. Cathy quietly and unobtrusively organizes the classroom. She sets out various activities and assigns groups of children to them. Eventually Cathy and Ann each sit at a table and help children as they construct the clocks. Cathy favours explaining and showing how to cut out with the children doing; Ann is still cutting out for the children.

The classroom has been organized by Cathy. Her takeover of the activities has been subtle; the students still appear to have public control of the class, as the next interaction illustrates.

Ann checks the time with Cathy. Ann stops the class working and initiates clearing up. Under Cathy's guidance the students have been focusing on giving clear instructions at such times.

## Theme 3: Team-teaching

*Observation 4.4   Mark with student teachers Alan and Mike*

Setting: Year 2 class

Alan settles the class as they come into the classroom. Mark is called out of the classroom. Alan directs the children, a table at a time, to sit on the carpet. Alan starts a 'holding' activity until Mark returns; he works with number bonds and the shapes of objects in the classroom. Mark returns and is ready to take over but waits until Alan turns to him.

Mark then says 'Now, are you going to show me how quietly and sensibly you can go back and sit in your places?' Mark starts his lesson on alphabetical order by asking five children to stand up. He repeats their names, stressing the surnames (Atkinson, Barnet, Bentley, Bradford and Claxton). He asks the children, 'Why have I picked those five?' Alan and Mike are observing. Mark continues explanation of alphabetical order and then explains the work the children have to do.

The children settle to work. The first task is to arrange groups of letters in alphabetical order. Mark, Alan and Mike all move around the room helping the children. Mark tells Mike and Alan that he is aiming for understanding today; it is not important that the task be completed.

Mark calls a group to the carpet and explains the second piece of work: placing a list of words in alphabetical order. The group returns to its table. Mark and Mike talk about how another group is coping with the work and discuss ways of helping them to understand.

## Theme 4: Contingent dialogue

*Observation 4.5   Mark with student teachers Mike and Alan*

Setting: Year 2 class

Mike is deciding which eight children to choose for his art task. Mark suggests taking Matthew: 'He is not very good at art but it will be good for him.'

Children enter the classroom and sit down in their places. Mark praises the behaviour of one table. When the class is quiet Mark explains what will happen this afternoon. He recaps the Easter story as far as the children have gone.

Mark hands over to the students. Mike takes his chosen group and Alan directs the rest of the class quietly to the carpet. Alan continues the Easter story from the point that Mark had reached. The children are absorbed by the story. Mark is observing both Alan and Mike.

Alan then explains a task that the children have to complete. It consists of ordering pictures that tell the Easter story. The less able children are to sequence the pictures and colour them. The middle group is to complete the sequence and move on to a cloze procedure sheet that retells the Easter story. The most able children are to sequence the pictures and then write the story in their own words. Once the work is explained, Alan directs the children back to their places. Mike's group continues with their artwork. Mark is observing and writing notes.

Alan's groups start their work. Alan checks that the support teacher, who is there for two children with severe learning difficulties, will assist all the less able children. Mark suggests quietly to Alan that it would be a good idea if the children put their initials on the back of their pictures once they have cut them out. Alan stops the class to issue this instruction. A little later Mark and Alan discuss how best for the children to organize the pictures in their books. Alan and Mark are moving around the room checking the children's understanding of the story. Both are asking questions such as 'What happened first? What happened to Jesus here? Can you remember the name?'

After the play-time break that follows the session, the head teacher takes infant assembly. Mark is allowed non-contact time here to discuss the day with Alan and Mike. Mark uses his written notes to give feedback.

*Observation 4.6   Sue with student teachers Rachel and Hilary*

Setting: Year 1 class

At the start of the session Rachel and Hilary are working with a group of six children each. The groups are mixed ability and the work is to contribute to mathematics assignments that have been set for the students by the university. Rachel's group is playing games with coins that necessitate exchange and decomposition. Hilary's group is comparing candles, judging the biggest and smallest, ordering them in size, and measuring them with blocks. Both groups are preparing for the class shop where the candles will be 'sold'.

Hilary has differentiated the task on which she is working with the children into three levels and the children work in pairs on the related but graded elements of the task. Rachel's work is differentiated by the amount of support she gives to each child. An additional support teacher in the classroom sits with the remainder of the class on the carpet and reads them a story. Sue is preparing for a painting activity and keeping a close watch on the students' work. Sue briefly talks to Hilary and the children in her group.

Twenty minutes after the start of the session Sue explains the morning's work to the rest of the class. She and the support teacher settle the class to work on a writing task or the painting activity.

Sue monitors all the children as they work. Rachel is experiencing difficulties with Jack, one of the pupils, mainly because the task is too difficult. The other children are coping very well but when Rachel suggests that Jack should just colour in the work sheet they are using rather than continue the mathematics activity, the other children declare that this is what they want to do too. The break-time bell intervenes.

During break-time Sue initiates discussion with Hilary about the mathematics work. They look at the children's work together and talk about their abilities and progress. Sue then talks to Rachel. Rachel raises the problems with Jack which they discuss. Sue praises the way in which Rachel is stretching the most able and suggests that she needs to plan specifically, not just through outcome, for the less able children in her group. Sue then briefly asks Rachel and Hilary about their future plans. Rachel and Hilary are planning to use a concept keyboard in the shop and Sue offers to help them programme the overlay at lunchtime.

## Implications of the case studies

It is clear that although the mentors we have discussed were similar in many ways, they were also at times strikingly different. What all of them were attempting to do, in different ways, was to enable the students to read the classrooms through the lenses of a more expert practitioner. They were highlighting for the students what was important in the teaching situation at the time. The intention appeared to be that the students would learn to identify key aspects of classroom life and react appropriately.

However the differences demonstrate that mentoring, like teaching, is not a set of simple skills, but is grounded in mentors' beliefs about teaching. Cathy, for example, had a much lower level of tolerance for student error than did Sue. Cathy intervened quite actively, while Sue, who also observed trouble brewing, gave students strategies for coping but did not intervene herself. Clearly mentors have to feel comfortable with the decisions they make while mentoring. Consequently it is important that the examples we have given are not used as yardsticks for the measurement of mentor quality but as starting points for the consideration of individual practice.

A good place to start on this, if you are a mentor, would be to recall a session in which you were working with student teachers or a single student in your classroom. List the learning outcomes that were intended for the pupils who were working with a student. Also list the intended learning outcomes for the student. What happened during the session? What did you notice that you felt the student was unaware of? Were you able to interact with the student while teaching was going on? Where you able to help the student see the situation through your eyes at any point? If you did not interact with the student, why not? Had you agreed that you would not intervene, but would do something else which would enable you to provide another form of feedback? Do you feel uneasy about intervening when students are teaching? How might you overcome that unease? Are there other factors that make interaction difficult? Can you overcome them?

Most of the questions in the last paragraph demand an examination of the organization of time and space in classrooms as another type of learner is incorporated into the dynamics at work there. For example, it may be appropriate to create time in teaching sessions for mentors to focus their attention on students. It may also require a consideration of the relationship that mentors have with students. If students are to be working in established classrooms as novice practitioners, there will need to be ground-rules which recognize that they are still learning to read the demands of classrooms and will require help in identifying what is immediately relevant. In addition, they may well need assistance in managing their response to it. However, as we indicated in Chapter 2, in their impatience to be the teacher some students may feel that helpful mentor support is an impediment.

Ground-rules may help clarify the situation. These rules will change as students become more competent practitioners. Nevertheless the right of a mentor to intervene with sensitivity as a kind of ghost teacher (for example Observation 4.1) may need to remain a feature of mentor scaffolding. If a mentor's responsive support is made explicit through the creation of a set of ground-rules, attention is brought yet again to the position of students as beginning practitioners and learners in classrooms.

The active mentors we have just discussed were frequently employing all four of the action themes that we outlined in the observations we have just provided. There were, however, lost opportunities for even more active forms of mentoring and the possible enhancement of student learning. Look, for example, at Observation 4.3. Cathy's work at reorganizing the classroom appeared to have been so unobtrusive that the students were unaware of her actions. In making sure that her actions were not noticed by the children in ways that might have undermined the students as teachers, it seems that she hid her actions from the students as well. Neither did she mention what she had done in her later conversation with the students.

In addition, the behaviour Cathy modelled in encouraging pupil independence and in distinguishing between children in the level of support provided, similarly went unnoticed. It may be that one impact of explicit ground-rules would be that students are advised to watch teacher behaviour and comment on it. As you will remember from the evidence we considered in Chapter 3, discussion of teacher performance was an extremely rare occurrence in students' conversations with their mentors.

We are clearly starting to suggest that overt modelling of teaching should be a continuous feature of active mentoring. Such a suggestion may extend notions of mentoring in ways that have quite considerable implications for the professional development of mentors, because it places the practice of teachers who are mentors under close scrutiny.

At this point our examination of the relationship between what goes on while teaching and what is discussed between student and mentor requires us to return to the framework offered in Figure 2.2 in Chapter 2. We have emphasized the importance of mentor scaffolding which aims to assist the performance of students as they work in classrooms in quadrants B and C. We have suggested that scaffolding by mentors should be contingent, i.e. reactive, where possible, in response to student need. In addition it should focus, to begin with, on highlighting in action what is important in the activity occurring around a student. The support may also be gradually withdrawn as well as supplied. This responsive form of mentoring demands watchful mentors.

Our initial observations (Collison, 1994), questionnaire data and interviews with mentors (Collison and Edwards, 1994), suggested that quite frequently mentors saw student teachers as another useful pair of hands in classrooms. Planning conversations, for example, revealed that mentors were treating the students as they would other adult helpers who gave them much-needed opportunities to give attention to specific pupil learning needs. Scaffolding the performance of students has the potential to make considerable demands on mentor time in classrooms. In these circumstances the argument for team-teaching becomes quite strong.

## Activities

1 Undertake a team-teaching episode with a student. In your reflective diary (see Chapter 1), note, on the left-hand page, what were for you important features of the three phases of planning, teaching and evaluating the session. On the right-hand page, comment on how you used each of these three phases to provide support for (i) the student's practice and (ii) the student's learning about practice. You may find that (i) and (ii) are not both evident at each phase.

2 How might Cathy have ensured that the students learnt from her unobtrusive interventions shown in Observation 4.3? Plan an evaluation session with the students drawing on the evidence available in 4.3.

## Further reading

Elliott, B. and Calderhead, J. (1993) Mentoring for teacher development: possibilities and caveats, in D. McIntyre, H. Hagger and M. Wilkin (eds) *Mentoring: Perspectives on School-Based Teacher Education*, London, Kogan Page, gives support to our emphasis on the differences in approach to mentoring that are held by mentors.

Yinger, R. and Hendricks-Lee, M. (1993) Working knowledge in teaching, in C. Day, J. Calderhead and P. Denicolo (eds) *Research on Teacher Thinking: Understanding Professional Development*, London, Falmer, provides a scholarly analysis of the working knowledge of teachers as it is put into action in classrooms. It develops a notion of *ecological intelligence* which is compatible with the idea of situated use of professional knowledge that we have been pursuing.

Tomlinson, P. (1995) *Understanding Mentoring*, Buckingham, Open University Press, provides a useful account of what he describes as 'Progressively Collaborative Teaching' (PCT). PCT occurs when a novice teacher works alongside a more expert practitioner who scaffolds the learning of the novice.

# RUNNING

# SEMINARS

**What is a seminar?**

This is a reasonable question. When is a conversation between a mentor and some students simply a mentoring conversation and when is it a seminar? As with most definitions some arbitrary distinctions have to be made. So here goes. A mentoring conversation is for our purposes a conversation that relates directly to practice by, for example, considering practical details of teaching and learning, or by encouraging the students to move a little beyond the immediacy of action so that they think about the wider implications of the professional decisions they make in classrooms. These conversations are frequently spontaneous and are usually related to planning or evaluating a set of classroom events that have been observed by the mentor and the students.

Seminars do have some of these qualities. They are certainly aiming to take the students' thinking on beyond the 'here and now' in order for them to consider the broader principles of practice that we might want to think of as a form of practical theory. They do, wherever possible, take as their starting points an example of practice that has been observed by at least one of the participants. However, seminars are also quite different from the kind of interactive mentoring conversation that takes place in order to shape the practice of individual students before or immediately after they have taken action in a classroom.

Seminars are not spontaneous. They are timetabled; participants have usually been working in separate classrooms and bring different experiences to bear on any discussion; seminars consist of teaching points that have to be made if the students are to experience the curriculum to which they are entitled; and seminar leaders cannot easily draw on experiences that have been observed by all the participants. In other words, they are contrived teaching events that need to be managed. Students expect teaching events that take place in universities to be contrived and directed at their own learning. However, they may not hold the same expectations of seminar activities that take place in schools, where they do not always see themselves as learners.

The mentors in the programme we observed rapidly identified the management of school-based seminars as the most difficult aspect of their roles. The university responded with a workshop on running seminars in which various teaching techniques aiming at ensuring student participation in seminar discussions were shared. However, student passivity is only part of the problem that faces mentors when they have to set up and run seminars in school. Another important key to successful seminars is to have some understanding of why they are needed at all. What purpose do they play in the professional development of student teachers? In this chapter we shall tackle the purpose of seminars before moving on to consider how to plan a programme and to offer some techniques for lively seminars.

## What is the purpose of school-based seminars?

What happens in a seminar that cannot happen in a mentoring conversation? We have already indicated that seminars are contrived teaching events that are not embedded in the here and now of immediate practice. They are semi-private or semi-public situations in which students can acquire the skills that enable them to talk about practice in ways that are intelligible to those who were not witnesses to the events. Students therefore need to acquire and to use the discourse of pedagogy in order to communicate their experiences effectively to others in the seminar group. Of course they may choose to reduce the intellectual demand of the seminar conversations by keeping discussion at the level of unsubstantiated assertions. The challenge to the mentor who is leading the seminar is to sustain the intellectual demands that are made on students and to ensure the use of public frameworks for discussion of practice. We shall return to this later when we look at planning for teaching points and maintaining focus through seminar sessions.

Seminars are therefore where students first begin to test out their own understandings of public knowledge about teaching. They can use seminars to consider the broad principles or theories they have encountered. They can test their loosely held theories against their own experiences and those of others. The others will include fellow students and the expert seminar leaders. The role of the seminar leader is therefore to create situations in which particular principles or theories may be discussed. But it is often more than this. It may also include the introduction of new conceptual frames for the examination of practice and critique by the students.

If we return to the framework for student learning presented in Figure 2.2, we are talking about the kind of activities that might occur in quadrants B and C as students connect their own private experiences with the knowledge frameworks shared by other practitioners and available in the published literature. We are clearly not proposing that seminars are information-giving sessions. Students should be expected to read in preparation for analytic discussion of information and not sit passively while information is communicated to them. In the model of active mentoring we are proposing, the active learning of students as they consolidate and connect their understandings in seminar discussions is an important element.

We have so far been emphasizing, as we have throughout the book, what and how students learn about teaching from an analysis of teaching. Seminars may in fact be situations in which a balance can be reached between learning from thinking about one's own practice and learning from a consideration of wider-ranging professional decisions. Seminars, therefore, may not always start from a discussion of 'practice as task implementation' but can be the situations where, for example, important value questions are debated. Topics here might include parental involvement, the role of worship, anti-racism and gender expectations. General questions of professionalism can be aired in ways that alert students to their roles as members of a school team. Students can be introduced to the purposes of appraisal and staff development in relation to their own competence profiling. Areas that remain problematic for schools can be demystified as professional doubts and concerns are shared. Pupil assessment and responsive action planning might be an example of such a topic. In Chapter 7 we discuss some of the topics that could be developed in seminars.

We are not, however, suggesting that seminars are used to tackle the kind of well-being or emotional support issues that are also an important part of sensitive mentoring. In Chapter 2 we proposed that they might best be dealt with in formally arranged circle time sessions where the ground-rules necessary for self-help group work are specifically agreed.

## How did the mentors cope with seminars?

The mentors on the programme we observed certainly did not enjoy running seminars. It was often difficult to find an appropriate venue and enough uninterrupted time. But the biggest problem was the one we identified earlier. There appeared to be some uncertainty over the actual purposes of seminars in relation to student learning and over how mentors might construct seminars that were aimed at allowing students to operate with fresh insights into practice. Analysis of tape-recordings of 29 seminars (average length 30 minutes) confirms that the mentors who were leading the sessions found it very difficult to present seminars which allowed students to make meaningful links between general principles and actual practice.

The seminar leaders in the study adopted a variety of coping strategies which enabled them to fill the allocated seminar time, but we have few records of the kind of learning opportunity we are advocating. The seminars that were recorded for us seemed to fall into four categories. These were 'wheel in the expert', 'bring and tell', 'let's get sorted' and 'I saw something interesting the other day'. We shall look briefly at each in turn.

### Wheel in the expert

These were seminars where the senior mentor had asked, for example, a curriculum coordinator or a member of the senior management team to present a session on a particular topic. The expert duly arrived and told the students a great deal. There was often little attention paid to student learning through, for example, any recognition of where the students were in their current understandings and range of experience. There was rarely the opportunity for students to do more than ask clarificatory questions. These seminars were as a consequence usually one-sided. In the following example, we follow a curriculum coordinator and the senior mentor explaining in great detail the organization of a published scheme of work. TM is the mentor, CC is the curriculum coordinator and ST a student teacher.

> *TM:* In Year 2 they carry on to Workbook 2. What number does Stage 1 go up to?
> *CC:* Stage 1 goes up to Book 6 or 7. In Year 2.

The students did ask clarificatory questions, for example:

> *ST:* So are you saying you don't use Workbooks at Key Stage 2?

But the conversations tended not to engage the student teachers in the sort of discussion that could lead them into consideration of wider pedagogic issues. For example, in this case the conversation did not include consideration of the rationale for using a published scheme, the good or bad points of any particular scheme, or effective methods of teaching with a scheme. We suspect that the difficulties lay in the fact that the purpose of the seminar as an opportunity for active student learning through discussion was not made clear. The experts we tape-recorded appeared to feel that they had to pass on as much information as possible. It was little wonder that the mentors perceived student passivity to be a problem in seminars. Wheeling in the expert had many similarities with the next category of seminar coping strategy: 'bring and tell'.

### Bring and tell

Seminars that fell into this category could be recognized at a glance when we picked up the transcripts. Page after page of mentor talk told us that what was being offered here was a mini-lecture on a curriculum policy document or a set of resources. Mentors appeared to recognize, quite rightly, that they had been asked to take on the role because of their expertise and 'what they had to offer students'. However, very few had taken one step back to see that a simple transmission of their own knowledge was not necessarily the best way of ensuring that students learnt from them.

If we return again to Figure 2.2 in Chapter 2, what seemed to be happening in these seminars was that students were introduced to new information, a quadrant A activity, and expected to be able to work with it, a quadrant D activity. They were operating entirely in the intermental plane without any opportunity for testing understandings and consolidating their partially grasped conceptions in, for example, structured activities designed to give them the chance to use the language associated with the new ideas and to relate the ideas to their own experiences. In Figure 2.2 these activities would fall in quadrants B and C. They do not occur naturally; rather, they need to be planned for. In other words, situations for student learning need to be contrived within the structure of a seminar session. We shall return to this later in the chapter.

### Let's get sorted

Some of the mentors in the study filled seminar time with administrative issues. One example from our study records a seminar leader spending 45 minutes on the negotiation of the topics for the next two seminars! This negotiation did not include arranging any preparation that the students might undertake for the next sessions. Consequently the subsequent seminar presented the mentor with exactly the same difficulties. She had to take full responsibility for filling the time allocated to the seminar and again decided to use the time for organizational matters.

The use of seminar time for matters of clarification was quite common. We began to wonder whether much of the kind of conversations we were witnessing could have been replaced by the use of an ITT notice board in the schools. Again what was happening here was the transmission of information which could perhaps have been communicated in other ways.

We have already indicated, drawing on the work of Doyle (1986), how learners like to reduce the intellectual demands of teaching opportunities. The students certainly did not object to sessions that focused on the administration of their training programme. They in fact had a great deal to offer in those situations. They were often operating as the major conduit between the school and the university and used those sessions to pass on information from higher education tutors. There is clearly a lesson to be learnt for higher education here.

*I saw something interesting the other day*

These were indeed interesting sessions. Here the seminar leaders took as their starting points observations they had made in students' classrooms. They then developed particular teaching points from those observations. The following examples illustrate the strategy.

> Something that occurred to me as I was going round, I think it was with you, Jenny. You were asking the children about if there wasn't any bullying, and you said, 'What would you feel like if there wasn't any bullying?' and they said, 'Not happy.' I think you thought, at first, as I did, that he was being cheeky, a bit sarcastic, but I think that it is this idea of negatives that they can't handle.

And:

> Do you realize what you did that sorted them out? It really is very interesting to sit back as an observer. She really was very good with them. She didn't want them to call out and she was trying to remind them what she had talked about last week, 'Why mustn't you call out?' and of course they all called out why you mustn't call out! Eventually she got to the point where most of them put their hand up but one boy wouldn't stop speaking and you got really firm with him. You changed the tone of your voice, you changed the way you looked at him, you fixed him with a stare and there was no doubt. He was fine after that. From that incident remember, eye contact, change your facial expression, change the tone of your voice, you don't have to shout, but change the tone.

One nice element in the way that the seminar leader handled the introduction of these topics was the positive tone she employed. The second extract goes further and shows her celebrating a student teaching triumph. But as we said, these are only starting points. Seminars need to be structured so that students are allowed ways of engaging with the topics that are being introduced. The focus in the teaching session, we would argue, needs to move away from mentor as expert who can offer well-founded principles of practice when interpreting classroom events. The focus has to be students' learning and the role of seminar leaders has to centre on the management of that learning.

## Managing the learning of students

As we have indicated, managing the learning of students is not an easy task for mentors. Simon, one of the mentors in the study, did have considerable success in doing this in the seminars he ran. He started out with some chance of success by expecting the students to prepare for seminars. In the extracts that follow the students had prepared by completing similar tasks with their groups of children. As an example of peripheral participation, the tasks had been planned with Simon's support and provided a vehicle for the student teachers to work with a small group of children in order to explore the children's moral thinking. The seminar was planned to examine issues of moral development.

Simon opened the seminar by directing the students into small discussion groups:

> Can we quickly split into groups? I think if Janet, Mandy, Judy and Steven form one group, and Mark, Sarah, Joanna and Dave a second that gives you all the chance to talk to people with experience of different age groups. You should be able to get a feel for the way in which the idea of right and wrong develops and we'll come back together a bit later.

When the students came back together Simon managed the transition to continue the discussion in the whole group by asking Mandy: 'Was there anything in your group that you thought we'd all be interested in?' The comments that Mandy offered took the discussion towards a consideration of the student's performance as teachers within the task and after a few moments Simon interjected: 'I really meant, what about this idea of moral development? Did their attitude to morals surprise you? Did you feel their general idea of morals was what you would expect or . . . Judy?'

Simon continued in this fashion, occasionally asking questions: 'Did anybody feel that perhaps the children were saying what they thought you wanted them to say?' His actions can be described as those of a facilitator, guiding the discussion. Most noticeably he did not act as the source of all knowledge. He did not tell the students about children's moral development. At the end of the seminar Simon directed the students to their common task for the next seminar:

> I want you to do a maths task. It can be your own choice from the ideas in the booklet, or adapted from the booklet if your classteachers want you to do something slightly different, but maths please. I've arranged for Margaret who is the maths coordinator to have some release time so that she can spend some time coming round to observe you and then she will join us in the seminar.

There are several features of Simon's seminar that are worth further examination. Let us first look at what he did do and then consider some of the things he chose not to do.

- He planned a topic for the session.
- He asked the students to prepare for it by undertaking a specific task in their classrooms.
- He organized small group discussions so that the students could share their observations in safe semi-private situations.

- He kept the discussion to the agreed focus.
- He used questions to redirect students to the focus he wanted to pursue.
- He ensured that all the students had an opportunity to speak.
- He set the preparation task for the next session.

He was clearly acting as a facilitator for student discussion and was evidently highly successful in doing that. He had overcome the difficulties involved in working in seminars with the quite disparate classroom experiences that students bring and was setting up situations where students could learn from the experiences of others. In addition, by demanding that students step back from a discussion of task implementation he was legitimating their peripheral participation in the classrooms in which they had been placed.

What was he not doing? He was not introducing the frameworks that are publicly available in the field of children's moral development, for example Kohlberg (1975) or Gilligan (1982). He was equally not offering his own 'rule of thumb' frameworks or principles of practice. He did not therefore take the students' discussion beyond an examination of their own practices. It was not surprising that they wanted at times to steer the discussion to the task and its implementation. There was a focus to the seminar, but it might have been difficult to talk with any confidence of the achievement of specific student learning outcomes. A short paper or chapter on children's moral development as part of the preparation might have raised the intellectual demand of the seminar by requiring students to make connections between their own observations and the frameworks offered in the public domain.

The topic of moral development is a rich vein for student sceptical reading of the research literature. So much appears to depend on the culture in which the children have been raised, on their age and their gender. From there, discussion might range to similarities and differences between the values of home and school, the purposes of schooling and the responsibilities of teachers in these areas. Moving away from a focus on practice to pay attention to the ideas that form the discourse of education would seem to be one important function of seminars. But such seminars require skilled and careful planning. We shall look now at planning, first by considering the planning of a programme of seminars and then by focusing on the detailed planning of specific sessions.

## Planning a seminar programme

There is obviously a tension between the need to respond to concerns that arise in the course of time spent by a group of students in a school and the need to ensure that students receive the curriculum to which they are entitled as trainee teachers. This tension is evident in the seminar leadership strategy we identified as 'I saw something interesting the other day'.

Starting points of the kind we discussed under that heading need to be carefully managed into a coherent programme for students.

We do recommend that mentors who are responsible for seminars in schools plan a complete programme at the outset so that student learning can be given some coherence through a well-thought-out sequence of experiences. Partnership programmes may offer less scope for creative programme planning because partner universities may have a programme they want students to experience. However, if partnerships are to be partnerships and not colonization it may be appropriate for schools to assert their own parameters for a student seminar programme.

Let us therefore consider what those parameters might be. First, students are very likely to benefit from involvement in school-based INSET sessions that are arranged according to the priorities agreed in the annual strategic planning of schools. Students may need some preparation for their participation in these events and some structured opportunity for follow-up that differs from that required from school staff. The school's strategic planning may also drive the students' seminar programme in other ways. For example, if a curriculum coordinator is focusing on a particular curriculum development over one term, it makes sense to draw on that focus by incorporating it into the students' experience. Students could be asked to evaluate proposed new resources or could question the coordinator on his or her strategies for taking the new ideas into the classrooms of colleagues. Students could even become the vehicles that carry the new ideas and resources into the classrooms that are hard to reach.

Schools which tackle long-term planning as a team or even whole-school activity are particularly well placed to offer a framework for a student seminar programme. Specific priorities will be shared between teachers and will become the focus of discussions about resourcing and teaching at particular times in the school year. Consequently they can be built into the students' programme well in advance. Students gain because they are able to engage in discussions that ensure they see tasks for pupils not simply as an opportunity for teacher performance, but as part of a general curriculum entitlement that has to be planned for. In addition students are able to contribute to planning discussions in ways that develop their more general professional confidence and competence.

Mentors can benefit because when they work with students on planning they are able to combine their teaching and planning roles with their mentor roles. Taking curriculum planning as a starting point also eases the communication task of the senior mentor because teacher-mentors and students become involved in understanding the agreed sequence of student learning opportunities. As a result mentors are better placed than they might be to provide, with foresight, the kind of spontaneous interactive scaffolding for students that will prepare them for the future demands of their training curriculum.

In Chapter 9 we shall be suggesting that mentors and students can gain from jointly engaging in action-research-style examinations of practice. These enquiries may benefit from being incorporated into the strategic planning priorities of schools and individual teachers. The communication of an agreed timetable can assist the coordination of these activities to produce a well-supported set of learning experiences for students that can be consolidated in the seminar programme.

## Planning seminars

At this point we break our promise not to provide tips for mentors and present a few well-tested ideas. As contrived learning opportunities seminars need careful planning. We would not start a seminar without a draft time schedule organized in blocks of ten or 15 minutes or so. A schedule for a seminar on learning in groups might look like this.

12.10 to 12.15   Plenary: key concepts (from pre-reading) on overhead slide (language, structure, teacher time).
12.15 to 12.25   Groups of three identifying these key concepts and other features in their own observations of children working in groups.
12.25 to 12.35   Plenary: what did they observe? How does it fit the expectations provided by the reading?
12.35 to 12.40   Plenary: write on overhead what was not observed when comparisons are made with the reading.
12.40 to 12.50   Small groups: how might you set up tasks that meet the expectations? Plan a task.
12.40 to 1.05    Share the tasks and agree who will try and evaluate which task for the next session.
1.05 to 1.10     Catch up on administration or other issues.

The pace in this seminar is quite rapid and demands considerable preparation from all the participants. Preparation has involved both practical activities in the form of observation of children on task and reading about using group work to support pupil learning. The pace is sustained by a constant flow from plenary sessions to small-group work and back to plenary sessions where all are expected to contribute. The session concludes with a request that all participants undertake a small piece of action research where the theories available in the public domain are tested in practice.

The tricky element in the schedule we have outlined is the management of student learning while they are working in small groups, in order to ensure that what emerges from those group discussions provide the starting points for the learning outcomes one hopes to achieve in the seminar. We shall look at several tried and tested strategies that can be quite easily used in schools.

*Talk among the flip charts*

This activity aims at students being able to talk as they think, drawing on their own experiences and learning from each other. The final product is a number of pieces of flip chart paper attached to a wall. The sheets are covered in comments written by individual students. The comments may be confirmatory, they may raise questions, they may be contradictory. Whatever they are, they provide useful starting points for teaching for the seminar leader because they are drawn from the experience of the group and are displayed so that all seminar participants are working with the same text in the discussion that follows.

We shall illustrate the activity by taking the group task we have just outlined in the draft seminar schedule. The follow-up seminar might incorporate an activity that goes like this. Take five sheets of flip chart paper for each group of four or five students. If you are short of wall space you could manage with five sheets for up to eight students. Write one of the following headings on a piece of paper so that you end up with five sheets, each with a different heading.

- What I expected to see (column one) and hear (column two).
- What I saw (column one) and heard (column two).
- What I think the children learnt.
- What I did (column one). What I think I should have done (column two).
- What I have learnt.

Fix the papers in that sequence to a wall and give each student a large felt-tipped pen. Allow about 20 minutes or so for them to wander around and write their responses on each piece of paper. Stress that there are no right or wrong answers and encourage them to talk to each other. If you have also done the group work task you could join in with your own written comments. Make sure that you indicate that you too have learnt from the exercise.

When 20 minutes have passed, gather the group together and start a plenary discussion of each sheet. Start by working with what is there and then move on to raise the intellectual demand of the activity by, for example, questioning assumptions that lie behind some of the comments. This is a very flexible framework for focusing student talk and subsequent plenary discussions. The headings on the sheets can vary according to the intended learning outcomes of each session.

*Concept mapping*

You will be familiar with this activity with children in science activities. It can be easily applied to an examination of the pedagogic discourse that students need to acquire. Students could take a word, for example motivation, and create individual concept maps, compare their maps in twos or threes and look at similarities and differences. Key elements could then be shared in a plenary session that allows students to see that motivation is a complex construct. This discovery could be a precursor to setting a reading and an observation task for the next session.

### Organizing student thinking

Because of the busyness of school life, students can find themselves taking a lot for granted without considering the implications of professional decisions. It may be appropriate, for example, for students to consider the purposes and implications of encouraging parental involvement in pupil learning. This topic could be tackled initially as a paired SWOT analysis task. Here students would be provided with a proforma that consisted of a page folded into four quadrants which were headed in turn: Strengths, Weaknesses, Opportunities and Threats. They could then be asked to write their opinion of what enhanced parental involvement might mean for this particular school under those headings. After ten minutes analyses could be shared in groups or pairs and key topics brought forward to a plenary discussion.

Diagrams which allow students to organize information into overlapping sets can be completed in groups of three or four. They are useful ways of organizing students' thinking. You might want to ask students to consider the key concepts to be passed on to children in specific subjects. You could select subjects that are often taught together in umbrella topics such as geography and history. Students expect considerable overlap in the concepts employed but soon discover that differences can be quite stark. This activity can then become a starting point for an informed critique of topic work or a session on long- and medium-term planning.

### Working with resources

'Bring and tell' sessions can be very useful for students: but only if they are structured so that students can engage with the resources that are brought. Advance preparation is important. Curriculum policies can be circulated for prior reading and students invited to produce a number of questions. These might include how the document deals with differentiation or assessment. The seminar leader should indicate whether students' questions should focus on curriculum development planning and staff development or on the subject content of the policy. Again some additional reading from the research or professional literature should help to focus the thinking of students and raise the challenge of the seminar.

Resources for teaching can be offered to students for their evaluation. Students can use seminar time to examine the resources and to identify the criteria against which they will evaluate the resources in their own practice. If students are not able to use the resources, they could use the questions in a plenary session in which they interrogate the lead mentor over his or her experience or expectations of the resource.

## Leading seminars

We are suggesting that seminars require as much orchestration as most classroom teaching sessions. Yet seminar leaders are without the contextual support that well-planned classrooms provide. We shall conclude with a few tips that can make the running of seminars less of a strain.

### *Place responsibility on the students*

Establish and stick to ground-rules that demand that students prepare for sessions. Ensure follow-up where it is necessary by setting tasks, for example the evaluation of a teaching strategy, that are to be discussed in the next session. Do not feel obliged to be the source of all knowledge but use your knowledge to direct student contributions.

### *Collect short sharp readings*

Build up a small library of short readings that you can lend to students in order to raise the intellectual demand of seminars and to allow students to connect their private understandings with the frameworks that operate in the public domain. Harass tutors in higher education for help here. Most will have collected a useful stock for their own use or will be able to direct you to likely collections of papers or journals.

### *Keep your colleagues informed*

Let colleagues who are acting as teacher-mentors know what the priorities for student learning are over several weeks. They are well placed to help prepare students for their active involvement in seminars by giving the kind of contingent support that highlights particular aspects of practice.

### *Be willing to learn yourself*

Our own experience of the seminar activities we have outlined is that we learn a great deal from them. They all have quite important diagnostic potential and constantly keep us alert to the alternative ways of seeing that emerge in the responses and discussions. Our own preconceptions are frequently shifted and our teaching adapted as a consequence. So even though we have been emphasizing structure, we have in mind a flexible structure. What is of primary importance is the development of student thinking and understanding.

wealth of material that is now available, particularly in the fields of science and mathematics.

What a large number of studies indicate is that learners often bring commonsense and idiosyncratic understandings to areas of activity which experts in the subjects would see as demanding specific and shared ways of understanding, acting and recording. One example of the difference between idiosyncratic personal and public shared subject knowledge is the fascinating study of child street traders in Brazil (Carraher *et al.*, 1990).

The children who were studied worked as street traders for their families by selling fruit. They had an average age of 11.2 years. The children performed quite complex transactions while trading but did not use the formal rules of mathematics. The personal rules that they created worked well in the street but were heavily dependent on the context of transactions over coconuts. In classrooms the children were unsuccessful at tasks that were presented to them in decontextualized ways. The following example from the work of Carraher and colleagues demonstrates this.

*Male (12 years old)*

*Informal test*

*Customer:*   I'm going to take four coconuts. How much is that?
*Child:*      Three will be 105 plus 30, that is 135 . . . one coconut is 35
             . . . that is 140!

*Formal test*

Child resolves the item $35 \times 4$ explaining out loud 4 times 5 is 20, carry the 2; 2 plus 3 is 5, times 4 is 20. Answer written is 200.

(Carraher *et al.*, 1990: 213)

This study raises some important questions about the purposes of formal education. Given that entitlement to a curriculum that empowers learners is a prerequisite of current education provision, it would seem that access to the powerful publicly understood ways of thinking about, doing and recording mathematics, for example, is a child's right.

When issues of entitlement are translated into terms that relate to pupils' learning, we can argue that teachers have a responsibility to ensure that children are able to move from their idiosyncratic understandings to those that are publicly valued and used. Pupil empowerment through mastery of the publicly valued curriculum comes not only from their ability to communicate their understandings to others but also from the fact that the skills and concepts that are carried in the curricula are tried and tested and provide the building blocks from which children can become increasingly proficient. It was clear in the street trading example we discussed earlier that the street trader curriculum was well-matched to immediate needs but offered little preparation for moving beyond the demands of the fruit market context.

Studies like that of Carraher *et al.* highlight important features of subject knowledge. They tell us that subjects have their own languages to which specific meanings are attached: for example, *state* does not mean the same thing in both science and history. We can begin to see that specific forms of enquiry are associated with particular disciplines: for example, the processes of enquiry in mathematics are different from those in history. We are also able to recognize that subjects consist of sets of related and nested key concepts: for example, *faith* and *God* are basic concepts in religious studies and without a grasp of how these are understood by other experts in the subject area one would not be operating within the subject.

We have just described what is often called the 'discourse' of a subject (Edwards and Knight, 1994). At the same time we have suggested that one can operate within or outside a discourse, but that operation outside the discourse indicates a reliance on commonsense and usually limited understandings. Clayden and her colleagues (Clayden *et al.*, 1994) explored the notion of discourse as a set of shared understandings held by experts, in their case in mathematics, and talked of the need for an authentic mathematics curriculum through which children work 'at the heart of mathematics' and discover its power. They argue, therefore, that learners need to be brought in as participants in the real discourses of the subjects that make up the mathematics curriculum. Participating in the discourse involves learners in working as mathematicians so that they can be inducted into the culture of mathematics and its language. We have already suggested an equivalent process when we claimed that the main role of mentors is to bring student teachers into eventual full participation in the discourse of professional practice as teachers.

Edwards and Knight (1994), in their discussion of discourse and subject knowledge in early years provision, laid great emphasis on the acquisition and use of the language that carries the key concepts of a subject, for example division in mathematics, in contexts that make the meanings clear to children. They emphasized the importance of pupil–teacher interactions and of the tasks that take children into the use of a discourse as they think and work within the subject. Edwards (1994a) particularly stressed the use of groupings of children for the stage at which elements of a discourse are tested and internalized by children.

One challenge to primary school teachers is therefore to help children to make the shift from idiosyncratic ways of thinking which may limit their future learning. Having made this shift, pupils start to use those ways of understanding that are in operation within the discourses of the subjects that make up the curriculum. We of course recognize that the school curriculum itself requires considerable and constant debate.

Classroom tasks seem to have a pivotal role to play in the achieving of that shift. A great deal rests on them, as they not only carry the opportunity to work at activities that would be recognized as science by a scientist, for example, they also need to be structured to ensure that children are working at them as scientists. We are aware from data collected by science specialist colleagues (Riggs and Hayhurst, 1995) that students enjoy carrying out science activities with primary school pupils but often shy away from moving the children on to writing up the activity, however inventively the writing-up process might have been designed. There may be questions there about students' ability to move on from the fun of the activity, where commonsense understandings might be sufficient, in order to engage with an analysis of the science components of the activity when they ask pupils to record their experiences.

We are clearly not attempting to oversimplify the demands made upon primary teachers as they deal with the vast range of demands of the national curriculum. Nor are we suggesting the introduction of subject-specialist teaching from reception class to Year 6 across the curriculum. We find ourselves more in accord with the view presented by Alexander (1995) when he suggests that schools should analyse the educational functions that are required from staff, identify the expertise that is required and create a 'profile of professional roles which match them as closely as possible' (p. 296). Yet we are suggesting that some teachers will be more expert in some areas of the curriculum than in others and that specific expertise will not be spread evenly across a staff group.

We have already mentioned the use of curriculum coordinators in school-based training and shall return to the topic in Chapter 10. Mentors can as a consequence usually draw on a wide range of curriculum support for students and do not have to present themselves as the fully-rounded expert to the students with whom they are working. However, there still remains the question of what students are learning about subject knowledge as they create and implement tasks for children. We discussed the work of Shulman (1987) in Chapters 2 and 3. His notion of the amalgam of knowledge of what is to be taught and knowledge of pedagogy as the particular strength of classteachers is once again helpful. The amalgam of these elements allows us to begin to see that when, for example, expert generalist teachers think about subject knowledge in history, they are not doing so as expert historians. However, they do know that two key concepts in the study of history are time and evidence, and that ways of enquiry in history involve the analysis of evidence within temporal contexts. They also know how to stage the pupils' introduction to an acquisition of these concepts through a range of teaching and class management techniques.

Expert teachers are therefore expected to be experts in the transformation of knowledge of a subject into an opportunity for pupils to be inducted into it. Teachers will, of course, have their own ways of doing this with consequences for the relationship between mentors and students. Work on subject mentoring in secondary schools, for example Rodd (1995), raises interesting questions about how mentors perceive their specialist subject and as a consequence introduce the related pedagogy to student teachers.

Quite clearly the field of subject mentoring will be a fruitful area of research over the next few years, and one to which primary school-based mentors can make useful contributions. In our study we began only to scratch the surface of the topic. But in doing merely that we found much that provides food for thought.

## How students used tasks in classrooms

Over the three years of the research study of how students experience school-based training, students were observed as they worked with children in classrooms. The greater part of the observations took place while the students were placed in classrooms in pairs with one mentor for each pair of students. The object of these placements was to give the students the opportunity to implement tasks for pupils that had specific curriculum focuses. The pupil tasks were regarded as ways of following up curriculum studies sessions at the higher education institution. It was expected that the time spent in school on these tasks would contribute legitimately to the specified curriculum hours for each subject demanded by the training programme. Task implementation was once again pivotal to the students' learning experience. This time, student coverage of their own curriculum was the central issue, at least for those who designed the curriculum.

The observations that were made during the research study captured what the students were doing as they took pupils through the tasks. Thirty-four hours of minute-by-minute descriptive observations were analysed in order to reveal the curriculum focus of the tasks that were being implemented (Collison, 1995). In addition to making the observations, we asked the students and their mentors to identify the curriculum focuses of the tasks that were planned.

The data analysis involved working with expert judges in order to establish the curriculum subject focus of the activities that were observed as the students put their plans into action with pupils. The observed focus of each task was then compared with the stated curriculum intention. Three categories of 'match' between intention and outcome emerged. The three categories were: firstly, match of intended subject focus and evidence of subject transformation in the task; secondly, match of focus and task but a 'busy' activity only; and, thirdly, no match.

Table 6.1 gives a picture of the extent to which there was a match between student intentions and actual outcomes in task implementation. The analysis reveals a quite striking mismatch in science between focus of the tasks when implemented by students and students' intentions for the tasks prior to implementation. Only 17 per cent of the activities as they were observed in classrooms were categorized as science tasks by the expert judges. Other areas of noticeable mismatch were religious and moral education and geography.

Many students were quite clearly taking refuge in the mechanics of the

*Table 6.1* The match between students' intended subject focus and the content of observed tasks

| Subject | Category 1 Match (%) | Category 2 Match (%) | Category 3 Match (%) | No. of teaching sessions |
|---|---|---|---|---|
| Mathematics | 51 | 11 | 37 | 35 |
| English | 65 | 27 | 8 | 37 |
| Science | 17 | 9 | 74 | 35 |
| History | 67 | 6 | 27 | 15 |
| Geography | 48 | 24 | 29 | 21 |
| Art | 60 | 40 | – | 15 |
| R and ME | 41 | 48 | 11 | 20 |
| IT | 100 | – | – | 3 |
| PE | 100 | – | – | 1 |

*Key:*
Category 1 Match: Match of intended subject focus with the experience offered to pupils and evidence of subject transformation in the task.
Category 2 Match: Match of intended subject focus and task, but a less cognitively demanding activity than originally intended.
Category 3 Match: No match between intended subject focus and the experience offered to pupils.

tasks that they were setting. They were providing no evidence of the transformation of subject knowledge into a task that was designed to enable the children to work with an aspect of the discourse of the subject. Examples here included students who made silhouette pictures without attending to the original subject intentions of reinforcing the concepts of opacity and transparency. There was a strong tendency, for example, for science tasks to become exercises in manipulation skills involving cutting and pasting or colouring activities. There was also clear evidence of this tendency in other curriculum areas and particularly in religious and moral education, in history and in geography.

Other students were attempting initially to engage with the intended subject focus of the task they were setting, but appeared to slide away from direct engagement with the discourse at some point in the implementation of the task. While working with mentors in an action research project that aimed to develop subject mentoring in primary schools, Maynard similarly found that students' activities easily became superficial and trivial (Maynard, 1996).

One example from our study was the student who started to introduce a group of six reception class children to the principles of electrical circuits through an exploration of torches and their batteries (see Observation 6.1). The task started as one that appeared to be transforming scientific knowledge for the children but became dissipated into a cut-and-paste activity with no language reinforcement.

*Observation 6.1   Clare and six pupils*

Setting: reception class

Clare settles the children around a table and hands out two torches: one torch between three pupils. She asks the children to try to make the torches work. One does not work and she asks them to try to find out why it is not working. The children discover that it has no batteries. Clare provides batteries. She stops the exploration of the torches when one child asks if she may take out the bulb. She removes the torches and shows the children bulbs, wires and batteries and tells them that they have all that they need to make their own lights.

Clare gives each pair of children a battery and a bulb in a bulb holder. She shows them the wires with crocodile clips and explains how the clips work. She distributes the wires. She then tells the children again that they have everything here to make the bulb light up. She asks them to join them together in a circuit. The children get to work.

Two of the pairs are surprised that putting both wires on one end of the battery does not produce a lighted bulb. Clare allows them to experiment for about three minutes and then tells them how to make a circuit. All the children make circuits.

Clare then removes the equipment and gives out a work sheet with the title 'electricity in our homes'. She also hands out pages from catalogues. She explains that the children have to cut out objects that use electricity and stick them on the work sheet in the right room in the house that is drawn on the work sheet. She supplies scissors and glue and the activity lasts for almost 20 minutes. It ends when the class-teacher organizes the preparation for dinner time.

There were students who managed to maintain a curriculum focus in the tasks they implemented. The extract that follows is an example of one such session and, like the previous example, takes understanding of circuits as a task intention.

*Observation 6.2   Val and six pupils*

Setting: reception class

Val settles the children around a table and tells the children that they will be looking at torches. She hands out two torches: one for every three children. The children look at the torches and all take turns under Val's guidance to switch them on and off.

She says to the children that she wonders what makes the torches light. Several children say it is the batteries. Val asks them to look inside the torches. The children unscrew the torches and remove the batteries. Val suggests that they test the torches without the batteries.

Val confirms that they all know now that torches need batteries to light up. She then asks the children what else is needed. She tells them to look closely at their torches. Jenny suggests a bulb. Val gives a bulb to each child and asks them whether they can see the little wire. She tells them that it is called a filament and that when electricity passes through the filament it glows very brightly and the bulb lights up.

She then tells the children that they will make their own lights and asks them what they will need. She gives prompts by asking what the torch needed to light up. The children ask for batteries and bulbs. Val gives them batteries and bulbs in bulb holders. She directs them to work in pairs to try to make the bulb light up. The children discover that they cannot.

Val tells the pupils that she thinks that they need something else. They need some wire. She hands out wires with crocodile clips attached to them. The pupils try to make circuits. Val watches and encourages different arrangements. She allows them to try various combinations for about eight minutes. At that point one pair is successful. She asks that pair to explain what they did.

The other children complete their circuits and Val shows them that they have made a whole circle. The teacher dismisses the class for play-time. During the break Val dismantles the circuits. On their return from play-time the children remake their circuits and record them as pictures.

In Observation 6.2 the task was implemented by a student in ways that stayed true to the key concepts to be acquired and employed by the pupils and to ways of enquiring and recording in science. Val kept close to the discourse of the subject as she worked with the young children, both in the language she used and in the processes of experimentation and recording that she allowed them to experience.

The transformation of knowledge into tasks is certainly difficult but evidently can be achieved by students. Successful transformation seems to demand that student teachers have a sound grasp of five aspects of teacher knowledge. These are, we suggest:

- knowledge of the curriculum so that objectives may be set clearly and in sequence;
- knowledge of the learners so that their misconceptions may be anticipated;
- knowledge of learning processes so that tasks may be structured to meet the particular learning needs of pupils (see Chapter 7);
- knowledge of resources so that their use may be maximized and their lack overcome;
- knowledge of the key concepts and ways of enquiry that are integral to the subject that is being carried in the task, so that interaction with the learners can highlight those aspects of the learning situation.

In addition these aspects of teacher knowledge are framed by sets of values and attitudes that represent teacher professionalism. These values and attitudes may include equal opportunities and attending to the needs of 'the whole child'. Pulling these features together is quite a tall order! However, all these elements lie at the root of sound task analysis. We shall be examining task analysis in Chapter 7. In this chapter we want to consider the role of mentors in assisting students to deal with the subject knowledge aspects of task-setting. We are particularly concerned here with the assistance that mentors can provide as students attempt to transform their own understandings into learning experiences for children.

The following extracts offer two quite different types of mentor support. Both extracts refer to planning for science sessions. TM is the teacher-mentor and ST is the student teacher.

*Extract 1*

*TM:* So you have got four science sessions?
*ST:* Yes.
*TM:* If you want to do your last two doing a Christmas card with the whole class, you could incorporate light and colour into that, couldn't you?
*ST:* Mm.
*TM:* And if you want to do something about mixing colours . . .
*ST:* Like this one?
*TM:* Yes. I mean literally mixing red and blue together to make purple . . .
*ST:* Oh right, yes. How to make lighter shades . . .
*TM:* Or making lighter or darker . . .

*Extract 2*

*TM:* Instead of just saying that you are going to make shadow puppets, make them check what things around them let light through and which ones don't. And the reasons why, for example, we have got these curtains in our classrooms. So there are reasons for things being opaque and transparent. And then go on to shadow puppets. So rather than saying 'Oh, let's make shadow puppets,' say, 'Well, look, by using something that doesn't let light through you can make shadow puppets.' It's really to make them remember. The thing is, by showing a purpose to it helps their memory.

The first extract is no more than a series of tips that focuses on the tasks that are being planned simply as activities that the children do. The second extract goes much further as the mentor is alerting the students to some of the elements of task-setting that are necessary if knowledge of the curriculum and knowledge of the subject are to be transformed into experiences from which children are to learn. In addition the mentor is attempting to move from the particular to the general by suggesting to the students ways in which children might organize their new experiences and remember the key aspects.

## Is too much expected of classroom tasks?

We have given considerable emphasis to tasks in our discussion of the transformation of subject knowledge. That is in part due to the fact that our observations focused on the implementation of curricular tasks during curriculum-based school attachments. In the training programme we studied, the tasks that students took into the schools acted as a form of linkage between the higher education institution and the classrooms in which the students operated. The attention to curriculum focus was consequently crucial if the students were to experience the teacher training curriculum they were required to receive. The 17 per cent hit rate of science tasks is certainly worrying in that context.

The mentors were informed of the curricular focus of each phase of the programme but were not always aware of the fine detail of student requirements. They all found ways of accommodating the students' needs as they were conveyed to them, but were rarely able to make them central to their own planning. Consequently the students did not see, as a matter of course, examples of expert practice in the areas in which they were attempting to operate. Some mentors did make a specific point of modelling practice by, for example, running a whole-class science session. When this occurred, the students valued the experience. But because the students were not often taking what Lave and Wenger (1991) describe as peripheral participant positions in the classrooms, the tasks and their implementation counted for a great deal. The position as teacher that students were constantly taking raised for us some questions about the implications for student learning of a training programme that so heavily relied on task implementation for a student's understanding of the complexities of a subject-based curriculum.

We shall, as we have already indicated, be looking at task analysis in some detail in Chapter 7. One important aspect of that analysis is to decide upon the purpose of a particular activity in relation to pupil learning. If we return to the framework for teaching and learning that is given in Figure 2.2 and use it to examine pupil learning, we can see several stages to the process of mastering an element of a subject. These stages may be identified as introduction (quadrant A); learners' reconstruction of what they already know to allow them to accommodate the new information (quadrants B and C); and practice or display (quadrant D). This analysis owes a great deal to Bennett *et al.* (1984) and their study of pupil learning in mathematics and English. The framework has been developed and related to the deployment of teachers' time in classrooms in both Edwards (1994a) and Edwards and Knight (1994) and is elaborated in the next chapter.

At the introduction stage of the learning cycle key aspects of tasks are highlighted through, perhaps, demonstration or guided exploration in which there is a high degree of language support provided by the teacher. In classrooms these teacher actions are often found in whole-class teaching sessions in which children are introduced to the key concepts to be tackled. At the reconstruction stage of pupil learning one often finds children engaged on tasks which have been designed or selected by teachers. These tasks are implemented because they transform the subject knowledge that is to be acquired into activities in which the children themselves can enter the discourse of the subject. Well-designed tasks highlight the concept to be acquired by ensuring that children's engagement is not impeded by, for example, their poor reading or manipulation skills. Teacher monitoring of children on these reconstruction tasks is important as the learners may require additional help. But the level of teacher–pupil interaction is lower than at the introduction stage of the cycle. At the final stages of display or practice there is usually little demand for teacher attention as children should not be placed on tasks of this kind until they reach a reasonable degree of competence in the skills and concepts that are being employed.

The use of tasks for children as a vehicle for student learning about the transformation of subject knowledge has advantages. The design and implementation of these tasks are clearly challenging. The focus on task-setting in the sessions we observed emphasized the reconstruction phase of the learning sequence which is where pupils as learners make sense for themselves of the information that is carried in tasks.

Arguably at that stage direct teaching is not the most appropriate form of interaction. Rather interaction should be responsive to perceived pupil need. However, many of the students who were observed were perpetually busy with the children as the pupils worked on the materials in which the tasks were presented. The emphasis on the mechanics of the tasks that were outlined earlier may have been due to the students' difficulties with the key features of the subject discourses. They may also, perhaps, be due in part to the students' need to *be* teaching at all times. The students seemed to be making their presences felt in tasks which, if they had been part of a single teacher, full-class session, would perhaps have required little teacher time. We return once again to the rights of students to participate peripherally at times in the dynamics of classrooms.

Peripheral participation, or a partial withdrawal from task implementation in ways that would allow observation of pupils on task, may help students to understand how pupils interpret the tasks. It may provide insights into the sense that pupils make of tasks in relation to the subject orientation of the activities. We found examples of mentor advice that focused on the transformation of subject knowledge. But we gathered, in the conversation data, no evidence of student evaluations of tasks that considered pupil engagement with the discourses of subjects. Consequently the students did not provide us with any evidence that they were learning general principles associated with the transformation of subject knowledge in the design and implementation of tasks.

In Chapter 3 we suggested that when students set tasks for pupils, some attention should be paid to what the students might learn from the experience. We argued that the negotiation of a focus for student learning as they worked on tasks with children would benefit the students as it would allow evaluation sessions to accommodate more easily the exploration and shaping of some principles of practice. Our analysis of the weak subject focus of the tasks observed in this study would seem to lend weight to this suggestion.

Another weakness in an over-emphasis on the implementation of tasks for children as a way of ensuring that students gain access to their own curriculum entitlement, is that there is far more to primary teaching than task implementation. Even if we limit our discussion to the national curriculum we can see that there are some areas that cannot easily, or at least only, be taught through the setting of activities for pupils. Literacy is perhaps one such area. It permeates the entire pupil experience and requires teachers to be ever alert to the need for a rapid response to a pupil's learning needs. It demands the kind of sensitive and often anticipatory interaction that distinguishes the expert teacher. This kind of interactive skill cannot, we suggest, be acquired only through the setting of literacy tasks.

As part of the programme we studied, students were required to complete a 'literacy log' in which they kept a record of their own experiences of knowing about, observing and engaging with the literacy support required by pupils (Crossman *et al.*, 1995). The log was divided into sections which included managing social contexts for learning, assessment and record keeping and reading to children. Each section listed key activities or areas of knowledge to be addressed by the students. Under 'reading to children' these included selecting appropriate material, gauging when to pause for talk with pupils and knowledge of genres.

The lists appeared to help the students identify the strategies they were using as they brought children towards literacy and gave them a focus for consideration of their own abilities to deal with the strategies. The log aimed at developing the students' awareness of themselves as learners in a complex area of the curriculum. In doing so it seemed to help them to become familiar with the discourse of literacy teaching. The tutors who produced the log argued that it was designed to enable the students to develop expertise in literacy teaching and not expertise in literacy itself. It aimed at helping them to transform the knowledge of literacy that they possessed into ways of assisting pupil learning of literacy.

The log seemed to be plugging gaps in a teacher training curriculum that focused extensively on the design and implementation of activities for pupils. It also appeared to be doing more than that by identifying the importance of the students' own awareness of their powerful role as interactive supporters of children's learning in a variety of contexts and ways. In Chapter 4 we discussed the value of contingent mentoring. Here we are indicating the need to ensure that contingent teaching becomes part of the repertoire of students as they deal with subject knowledge.

The ability to teach a wide range of subjects in the responsive manner we have just suggested does make considerable demands on the subject expertise of teachers. It would seem that an inevitable consequence of these demands will be that some schools will develop systems of subject-specialist teaching, at least at the end of Key Stage 2. However some schools may not be able to do so. Consequently an important lesson for students to learn is how they might learn from colleagues. The colleagues who will have most to offer, as students deal with the subjects of the national curriculum, will be the subject leaders or curriculum coordinators.

We shall be looking at the role of curriculum coordinators in Chapter 10 and will be emphasizing the importance of their contributions to the experience of students in schools. This importance lies not only in the expertise that subject leaders have to share, but also in their capacity to enable the students to learn early in their careers that it is all right not to know something. In the Lave and Wenger (1991) framework of a community of practice it is permissible to position oneself peripherally in some areas of the community and to move only gradually towards full participation. In Chapter 10 we shall return again to this topic when we consider mentoring in the learning school.

## Activities

1 In a planning conversation with a student, identify the intended subject learning outcomes for a group of pupils. With the student's agreement observe the student while she or he sets up the task with the pupils. Focus particularly on the student's language and the extent to which the language carries the key aspects of the subject intention of the task. Identify how the student highlights what is important for the children to see in the task. Share your notes with the student and identify strategies for the development of student performance. You could offer to model the strategies in the classroom and ask the student to observe you and discuss the observations before attempting another similar session with pupils.

2 Work with colleagues to identify five or so key concepts in at least three areas of the curriculum. The definition of a key concept is an idea without a grasp of which you would be unable to operate in the subject. Examples would be 'place' in geography and 'state' in science. Interesting discussions can arise when it becomes clear that 'place' in mathematics and 'state' in history carry very different meanings from their use in

geography and science. Plan a small cross-curricular topic for a specific age range. Note any potential confusions over subject-specific meanings of concepts to be offered in the topic. At the same time consider the demands of ways of enquiry and recording that maintain the integrity of subjects.

## Further reading

McNamara, D. (1994) Subject study in teacher education, in G. Harvard and P. Hodkinson (eds) *Action and Reflection in Teacher Education*, Norwood, Ablex, gives a considered coverage of current debates on the importance of subject study to the experience of teacher education students.

There are an increasing number of texts which address the teaching of the national curriculum subjects in primary schools. Two that focus on the early years of school are Aubrey, C. (ed.) (1994) *The Role of Subject Knowledge in the Early Years of Schooling*, London, Falmer, and Anning, A. (ed.) (1995) *A National Curriculum for the Early Years*, Buckingham, Open University Press.

The next text takes English, science and mathematics as its focus and covers the whole primary age range. Murphy, P., Selinger, M., Bourne, J. and Briggs, M. (eds) (1995) *Subject Learning in the Primary Curriculum: Issues in English, Science and Mathematics*, London, Routledge in association with the Open University.

Edwards, A. and Knight, P. (1994) *Effective Early Years Education*, Buckingham, Open University Press, tackles the challenges facing early years practitioners as they work with the National Curriculum and young learners. It particularly focuses on how young learners are inducted into the discourses of subjects.

A challenging perspective on how children learn to organize the world in which they operate is proposed in the following text. The ideas do not map neatly on to the National Curriculum framework. The study provides a useful starting point for speculations about the nature of children's minds and how they acquire formal knowledge. Karmiloff-Smith, A. (1992) *Beyond Modularity*, Cambridge, MA, MIT Press.

# PEDAGOGY AND
# INITIAL TEACHER
# TRAINING

## The challenge for mentors

Mentors are asked to work with student teachers because they have expertise to share. That expertise is grounded in the experience of teaching often gathered over a considerable number of years. In Chapter 2 we drew on the work of Shulman (1987) in order to examine the nature of teachers' pedagogical content knowledge which, according to Shulman, informs teachers' classroom decision making. We suggested that research on teachers' knowledge tells us that this is often held tacitly and is rarely elicited in the professional lives of teachers in schools. Furthermore, again according to Shulman, teachers' knowledge in action can be seen to be a well-combined mix of a variety of elements. These include knowledge about the content of the curriculum and knowledge about teaching and learning. These are the elements that students need to acquire while training so that they can mix their own blend of pedagogical content knowledge.

The major advantage of school-based training is that practical experience can be immediately connected to principles of practice as students and mentors work together in schools. In Chapter 3 we suggested that mentors can use planning and evaluation conversations to highlight particular principles as they emerge in discussions of practice. In Chapter 5 we indicated that school-based seminars may be appropriate contexts for overtly holding interpretations of practice alongside more widely held principles or theoretical frameworks for practice. However, in order to highlight or to provide opportunities for comparisons of local practices and wider principles, it is necessary to be able to call up, from tacitly held understandings, ways of representing these principles. In this chapter we shall not be drawing directly on data from the research project; rather we shall identify some of the pedagogical principles that have been evident in our discussions of classroom practices in the previous four chapters.

## Starting with planning

When students spend extensive periods in schools they are well placed to become attuned to the priorities and annual rhythms of planning and assessment that drive a school year. One of the major training experiences available to students in such situations in schools is to be able to work with experienced colleagues on long-, medium- and short-term planning. In addition, students are often able to see how these might be connected to the demands of pupil assessment and the action planning for pupils that can be associated with assessment. We shall therefore take planning as the starting point for a consideration of some of the key topics that mentors might be called upon to discuss with students.

We shall focus on short-term planning as it is here that the majority of mentor–student conversations will occur. Our data tell us that planning conversations tend to focus on the implementation of the tasks that carry the curriculum to pupils (see Chapter 3). In Figure 7.1 you can see a planning proforma that contains most of the features that need to be considered when students plan sessions. The conversations between mentors and students that we taped indicated that students emphasized tasks as activities that needed to be resourced in their planning. They appeared to pay little attention to the other aspects of planning that are shown in Figure 7.1.

The complexities of planning seemed quite frequently to be avoided by students as they started to think about their performance in classrooms. Our own experience is that the basic difficulty for students as they deal with short-term planning is the identification of intended pupil learning outcomes, for example *be able to distinguish between animate and inanimate objects*. Yet the definition of intended pupil learning outcomes is central to short-term planning, which must aim to transform the general curricular goals that lead long- and medium-term planning into activities from which children might learn. We shall pay attention to this aspect of planning when we look at task analysis in the next section.

Differentiation, which we have placed alongside learning outcomes in Figure 7.1, arguably may be too much to ask of students in the earlier stages of their training. However it may be worth raising it as a task design question even if students can only deal with it at the level of differentiation by outcome in some of the more open-ended tasks that they set. Its

| Curriculum area (from programmes of study) | Intended pupil learning outcomes for groups/class | Differentiation within groups/class | Tasks and resources | Teaching focus | Use of teacher time | Assessment opportunities |
|---|---|---|---|---|---|---|
| | | | | | | |

Figure 7.1  A proforma for planning half a day's work

inclusion at the task design stage of planning reinforces the need for students to start to plan from the perspective of pupils as learners.

The columns in Figure 7.1 that demand an analysis of teaching focus and the use of teachers' time alert students to their own importance as a resource for pupils and at the same time should take them to a consideration of the appropriateness of their teaching interventions in relation to pupil learning needs and desired task outcomes. Assessment opportunities are included as a reminder of the relationship between planning, pupil performance and unobtrusive teacher assessment of pupil performance. The wide column headed 'tasks and resources' is of course a central component of any planning schedule, but comprises, as this proforma indicates, only one aspect of the complex process of planning for pupils' curricular learning. Each of these columns leads to important pedagogical questions. We shall start to tackle these by looking at task analysis.

## Task analysis

Faced with a classroom of children, a school day and a curriculum to deliver, it is little wonder that, as Edwards and Knight (1994) put it, teachers measure out their days in pupils' tasks. Tasks ensure that children's activity remains under the control of the teacher. If experienced teachers think of their time in classrooms as a series of tasks that children will undertake, it is not surprising that students who have far less confidence about their ability to maintain control are heavily dependent on the implementation of activities as a way of maintaining some form of order in what they quite rightly perceive to be incipient chaos. The potential for chaos in classrooms where active pupil learning is occurring is the starting point taken by Doyle in his influential work on academic tasks and pupil learning (Doyle, 1986).

Doyle's work is important because it identifies the pivotal place of academic tasks in bringing together for teachers understandings of curriculum, children and classroom management so that the focus can be placed on the management of pupil learning. He also alerts us to the likelihood that what is offered to pupils in carefully worked-out tasks is not what children see when tasks are set. Consequently pupils work hard to turn the task into something familiar and manageable.

Building on years of classroom observations, Doyle argues that academic tasks for pupils have two dimensions: risk and ambiguity. Tasks that are low on both dimensions are frequently heavily structured routine tasks which do not stretch the pupils when they undertake them. Copying from the blackboard would be an extreme version of such a task. Conversely, tasks that are high on risk and ambiguity present opportunities for what pupils perceive to be failure. However these tasks contain the potential to stretch learners and to develop their ways of conceptualizing and acting on the world. Many problem-solving tasks would fit this definition.

Pupils in the majority of classrooms, however, fear the risk of public failure and consequent damage to their self-esteem that might come from tasks where they are uncertain about what constitutes success. Therefore they work hard to avoid risky and ambiguous tasks. In fact, argues Doyle, they do more than that and actively bid down the risk and ambiguity in the tasks that are set, so that they are transformed into easily managed routine activities.

When pupils bid down the demands that a task is making of them they tend to do it by negotiating increased amounts of teacher support until they reach the point where they are clear what the teacher wants from them and they know that they will be able to achieve the goals. Doyle argues that teachers in busy classrooms collude in the negotiation process because the last thing they want is the disruption that can be caused by children who are not coping with the activities they have been set. We discussed in Chapter 3 the process of negotiation that attempts to reduce the risk of failure in tasks, in relation to how students set about implementing the tasks for pupils from which they too are supposed to be learning.

There is a lesson here for how students set tasks in primary schools. Doyle's work is sensitive to the complexities of lively classrooms and the difficulties that pupils can experience as they interact with the vast array of stimuli that comprise most classrooms. He suggests that one important aspect of teaching is the identification and highlighting for learners of what is important at any particular point. It would seem that there is a great deal to be gained from identifying for pupils what it is they might be experiencing as they undertake a task. If we consider the first extract we discussed in Chapter 3, where the student and the pupils were apparently seeing a religious and moral education task as an art activity, we can see how valuable it might be, for both students and pupils, to identify what is to be highlighted in a task.

Pupils bring their own current understandings and expectations into the classrooms in which they are expected to learn (Schunk and Meece, 1992). These expectations and understandings are brought to bear as they start to engage with the tasks that have been devised for them. How pupils interpret classroom tasks is a relatively new yet important field of research. For example, whether pupils see a writing task to be about producing a page of neat writing, a lively and long story, or the correct use of the conventions of punctuation, are crucial questions for teachers who depend on tasks to carry the curriculum to pupils. The work of the PACE project in Bristol promises to be particularly fruitful here (Pollard *et al.*, 1994).

Research that has a slightly longer history suggests that not only is the interpretation of the meaning of the task important for the intellectual development of the pupils, but what is also of equal relevance is how pupils perceive what teachers believe to be commonly held understandings. Laurie Lee related the story of his disappointment on his first day at school. Having been told by his teacher to wait there for the present, he found that he had to return home without the gift he had been expecting ever since that instruction. This is a telling example of the intellectual misconceptions with which children can also approach curricular tasks.

Doyle's research has therefore told us that task-setting and implementation are crucial control features in classrooms and that 'academic tasks' are a complex area which if opened up can help us understand how we might endeavour to manage the learning of pupils. If we add the work of Norman (1978) and developments of this work by Bennett (Bennett *et al.*, 1984) and Desforges (1985) to Doyle's analysis we can begin to find a framework for understanding how tasks might be used to manage pupil learning.

Norman's work provided a way of analysing the intellectual demands of tasks. He identified a process of learning which, in the simplified version presented here falls into three stages for learners. First of all learners take in new information and simply add it to existing ways of understanding the world. Then in the second stage of learning the new information is incorporated into existing mental structures to the extent that existing ways of understanding are adapted to accommodate the new information. Finally, learners fine-tune their new understandings by building them into their general repertoires of thinking and behaving. These three stages can be mapped on to Figure 2.2 in relation to pupils' learning in classrooms. Stage 1 falls in quadrant A, stage 2 is represented by quadrants B and C and fine tuning occurs as learners move from quadrant C and work confidently in quadrant D. In Chapter 6 we described these three stages as introduction, reconstruction and practice or display.

Bennett and Desforges argued that Norman's work placed a fresh perspective on how we might think about the match between tasks and pupils as learners. Tasks need to be designed so that they do not simply carry the curriculum like some kind of all-purpose delivery van. Rather, at the design stage teachers have to consider where, in the particular cycle of learning in an area of the curriculum, a child or group of children might be. Bennett and Desforges' work on task-setting in mathematics and English in primary schools emphasized the importance of the diagnostic framework supplied by Norman. Tellingly, for example, they revealed a tendency in the classrooms in their study, for those children who needed a lot of time at stage 2 to be rushed on to stage 1 of the next curriculum target, with scant opportunity for the much-needed consolidation activities that comprise stage 3.

In practical terms, as we outlined in Chapter 6, a stage 1 activity may be the introduction of key concepts or ways of working in a subject through, for example, the exploration of artifacts in a whole-class session in which children start to work with the language that carries the concepts. This might be followed by tasks which have been designed to enable pupils to work in groups and use the language as they work with the artifacts, to talk about them and to start to record their responses. Stage 3 might occur in a whole-class feedback session and be further developed in project work that will require children to draw on these new skills and understandings.

Assessment is obviously an important feature of this view of task and match to pupil learning. We shall look at the recording of assessment of pupil progress later in this chapter. At this point we shall simply emphasize the need to incorporate a monitoring of pupils' progress as they are moved through the stages of learning that Norman presented. The final column in Figure 7.1 can be used to indicate how students might make judgements about pupils' learning in ways that can be incorporated into their teaching interactions with children.

## Scaffolding

As these judgements are made, students have to consider the amount of support that pupils require if they are to make sense of a learning experience. The notion of *scaffolding* is helpful here. The early use of the term 'scaffolding' was found in the work of, for example, Wood *et al.* (1976) in the field of developmental psychology. Wood and Middleton (1975) studied how mothers support the learning of 4-year-old children. They found that sensitive mothers who successfully helped their children as they engaged in a problem-solving activity with building blocks moved up and down a scale of control over the learning of their children in ways that were dependent on children's needs. The scale ran as follows:

- demonstration
- preparation for assembly
- pointing out the relevant materials
- giving specific verbal instruction
- giving general verbal prompts.

If a mother started with a low level of control by using general verbal prompts and this proved to be insufficient to assist children, the successful mothers became more specific in their instructions. If that strategy failed they would take more control by becoming gradually more involved in working with the blocks. Once they perceived that the children had begun to grasp what was required they gradually moved down the scale of scaffolded support. David Wood (1986) usefully makes connections between this study and the work of teachers in more formal classroom settings. There he describes 'task induction' as the primary scaffolding function and the *sine qua non* of effective teaching.

The work of Wood and his colleagues reminds us that teachers usually have goals in mind for learners. In addition it provides us with a way of examining the degree of support that students ought to be giving pupils as they learn and particularly as they work on curricular tasks. As Wood argues, teacher support ought to be contingent, that is, responsive to pupil need. Norman's stages, as we have presented them, imply a rigidity. Wood's work reminds us of the importance of contingent teaching however carefully we might plan.

Nevertheless we suggest that short-term planning can benefit from the perspective that Norman's work brings. This is particularly the case when we consider the amount of scaffolding from teachers that might be required at specific times in a teaching and learning sequence. In the first of the learning stages identified by Norman the need for scaffolding is extensive. In a classroom context teachers guide the attention of pupils to the learning focus of the task. In Wood's terms pupils are inducted into the task. At that point children are given specific prompts to enable them to draw on relevant previous experiences and they may be provided with a demonstration of how to tackle the tasks that face them at stage 2. At stage 2 teachers withdraw a little of the support so that the children are able to start actively constructing their own understandings. Careful monitoring at this stage will reveal the need to restore some scaffolding by, for example, help with mundane vocabulary, highlighting what is important in the task through specific questions or by the manipulation of materials. By the time pupils proceed to the final stage given by Norman they should require little teacher support.

By starting our examination of scaffolding with the work of Wood and his colleagues we have not taken into account the extent to which scaffolding can be built into the resourcing of a task. At a general level, a language-rich classroom can provide multipurpose learning support for pupils. At the specific task level, pupils can be directed towards particular ways of responding by the resources that are made available. For example in a box-making task the combination of banning Sellotape and providing rulers, squared paper, card, glue and opened-out small commercially-made packages will lead pupils to an exploration of the design of boxes and careful measurement of those that they make.

Another important aspect of task analysis is the identification of the aspect of knowledge that is to be transmitted in the task. We talked at some length in Chapter 6 of the need to transform subject knowledge in ways that maintain the essence of that subject. The essence, we argued, could be found in the subject-related talk in which the key concepts are used and in the methods of enquiry and representation that are part of the culture of a particular subject. However at this point we shall simply refer you back to Chapter 6 and our emphasis on the use of the discourse of a subject there. We shall now move from task analysis to consider its implications for classroom management.

## Managing the learning of pupils

### Using groups

Grouping in the majority of classrooms is a management device which often allows for differentiation by task. Placing children in groups does not necessarily lead to their cooperative learning and it is frequently not the intention that it should. However, research on children's classroom learning is beginning to suggest that children's exploratory talk while they are engaged in group work, of the kind we have been describing as stage 2 when we discussed task analysis, can assist their understanding (Phillips, 1985; Mercer, 1995).

Mercer defines exploratory talk as talk 'in which partners engage critically but constructively with each other's ideas'. Ideas are presented and maybe challenged, and challenges are justified and followed by alternative suggestions. Mercer argues that this form of talk between children on tasks makes their knowledge more 'publicly accountable'. Using Figure 2.2 in Chapter 2 such talk would fit quadrants B and C in a child's cycle of learning. It needs to be specifically encouraged and tasks need to be designed to allow it to happen. But it does appear that this form of pupil talk can enhance pupil learning. There are of course implications here for pupil groupings. A small-scale study by Bennett and Cass (1988) examined groupings in considerable detail and found that while the most able children fared well in any grouping, less able children did better when two less able children were grouped with one more able child than if they were grouped together or were a minority in a grouping.

The research on cooperative groups and pupil achievement is growing rapidly and appears to fall loosely into two categories. First of all there is the mainly North American work, for example Slavin (1990) and Johnson and Johnson (1994), which concerns itself primarily with the social interactions within groups and the extent to which cooperative group work can lead to efficient task completion. The second category draws more on UK research and tends to focus on how groupings can be used to enhance the learning of pupils. Representative work here, alongside that of Mercer, is Bennett and Dunne (1992) and Light and Littlejohn (1994).

Light and Littlejohn write from a background in developmental psychology and unpack the processes of children's learning in groups with reference primarily to cognitive psychology, though they are strongly aware of the power of social context in influencing motivation to learn. They make similar points to Mercer and emphasize the importance of a degree of conflict or differences in understanding within a grouping and the need for experience of giving and receiving explanations.

Bennett and Dunne take a related set of perspectives and embed them firmly in the processes that occur in primary schools. Bennett and Dunne conclude their study of teachers' use of groupings by suggesting that the following issues should be addressed when considering cooperative group work:

- the interaction between the social and cognitive intentions of the grouping
- the type of task required
- the match or appropriateness of the task to the children in the group.

Students could usefully be questioned on these issues whenever they suggest tasks for groups.

We find ourselves in sympathy with the idea of a group as an opportunity for talk which carries the discourse of a subject and hence enhances learning. It is central to the Vygotskian framework we have been pursuing and presents quite specific challenges to students as designers of tasks. Part of transforming of students' own understanding of an area of the curriculum into tasks for children, we would argue, has therefore to incorporate opportunities for task-related exploratory talk in pairs or small groups.

### Managing teacher time

Attention to pupil talk on carefully designed tasks raises the question of how students manage their own time to enable them to be a resource for pupil learning. When we discussed scaffolding in the previous section we talked of how teachers need to gauge the amount and type of intervention they make when working with pupils. We pointed out that although good teaching is as responsive to pupil need as it is possible to manage, when undertaking short-term planning, it is helpful to consider where, in the stages provided by Norman's analysis of learning, children's learning needs lie and what kind of activity they require. We then traced how the scaffolding provided by a teacher may be gradually withdrawn as the pupils become more firmly in control of their own learning. The major implication of this approach for student teachers is that having undertaken the analysis, they should be able to plan a series of activities which ensures that they are not required, for example, to be setting up two introductory activities for two groups at the same time.

Edwards (1994a) tackles incorporating the use of teacher time into planning for the management of pupil learning by suggesting that lesson plans indicate what degree of teacher intervention is likely to be required. A stage 1 activity will make high demands on teacher time, a stage 2 task will require watchful monitoring and a stage 3 task light monitoring. There are also implications here for classroom layout and the positioning of a teacher in the room. The degree of watchful monitoring required should indicate to students why they need to position themselves towards the centre of the classroom and where possible create a space within which they can remain mobile and consequently alert to all the actions of all the pupils.

Our emphasis on task implementation has meant that we have paid little attention to how students need to learn to create an active learning environment as a support for pupils. Examining the use of their time as a resource for the pupils as learners can lead students to discern which of their actions support pupil learning and which are mundane and could be replaced by a system that allowed the children to be more in control of their own learning support. Word banks and mathematics resource areas which children are able to use are examples of issues that students should be considering as they examine their own roles as valuable interactive resources for pupils.

## Pupil assessment

Students are often inducted into assessment of pupils by being asked to compile a child study. This exercise is certainly valuable. Not only can it develop the observational skills of students but it can be one element in the legitimating of their peripheral participation in classrooms. However, it will eventually be necessary to assist the development of their teacher observation skills by giving them a tight focus for observations. One way might be through their becoming familiar with some aspects of the code practice for the identification of children with special educational needs.

The focus that all will need to be able to deal with in their training is, however, assessment against the demands of the curriculum. So much has changed since the requirement for teachers' curriculum assessments was first presented to primary schools in the late 1980s that, at the time of writing, many schools are struggling to revise whole-school systems of assessment, recording and reporting. None the less students do need to be made aware of the processes of at least assessment and record keeping and should be able to relate them to planning for pupil learning in the core areas of the curriculum.

The three stages of learning we identified in the discussion of task analysis earlier in this chapter can again be called into use. As we suggested then, a child's progress through activities related to each of the three stages should depend on a teacher's assessment of the pupil's readiness to move on to the next stage. Consequently students' assessments of pupils should be able to pick up on whether a child has managed to demonstrate the desired learning outcomes of a particular activity.

The three-stage model allows students to recognize that some activities are intended merely to familiarize pupils with an aspect of the curriculum, some are intended to allow them to begin to make sense for themselves of a curriculum target and some are intended to allow pupils to demonstrate mastery of a target. If assessment is to be unobtrusive and built into a cycle of teaching and learning, students also need to recognize that they should not sacrifice valuable teaching time in order to carry out specifically designed assessments. The demands of heavy scaffolding in the early stages of a pupil's learning cycle mean that students will spend most time with pupils at that stage and less as pupils make progress towards mastery. Consequently students need to be focused in their assessments of pupils and be aware in advance of which aspect of pupil performance is likely to demonstrate successful completion of a particular stage in a cycle of learning.

Assessment is a demanding aspect of teaching. Consequently we suggest that students are brought gently to curriculum-led assessments by working with a limited number of intended pupil learning outcomes in one area of the curriculum and with very few children. Our own experience is that it is easier to start with mathematics or science than with English. Students can be given a recording framework that allows them to monitor pupil progress against a curriculum target through each stage of the learning cycle.

Three horizontal lines, one for the completion of each stage of progress through a cycle, against each curriculum learning outcome, for each child, would be a sufficient record. At the same time there should be space in any recording proforma for students to make comments about pupils' specific needs or accomplishments. Above all, students need to learn that records of this kind are working documents which are meant to lead their planning. Reporting is yet another stage and not one that they will usually have to deal with personally in initial training.

The use of three horizontal lines, or three different coloured dots, or whatever simple scheme of recording is selected, is particularly valuable when students reach the stage in their own learning where they have to deal with differentiation in task design. Differentiation may be tackled by students through the provision of additional interactive scaffolding, it may be built into the demands of tasks that are set for groups of pupils, or it may be handled by having open-ended activities that allow differentiation by outcome. However, if students are to take responsibility for ensuring that pupils learn and do not bid down the demands of tasks, they have to indicate their expectations of pupils' performances and ensure that pupils continue to progress through their cycles of learning. Becoming alert to how pupils perform through a limited amount of focused assessment can at least indicate to students the need to relate assessment to planning and to the expectations they hold for pupils as learners.

## Activities

1 Consider the last few activities implemented by students in your classroom. Then categorize them using:

   (i) *either* Doyle's framework of high or low risk and high or low ambiguity *or* categories that label the tasks as routine or challenging;
   (ii) the three-stage model of learning based on the work of Norman that we have been discussing in this chapter.

   (Note that tasks may be high on one of Doyle's dimensions and low on the other. For example, a tightly resourced, clearly focused problem-solving task which calls for pupil self-evaluation of outcomes against agreed criteria would be high on risk – the problem may not be solved – but low in ambiguity.)

   Observe the student as she or he implements another pupil task. Consider the extent to which, if at all, the task is bid down to a more routine and less intellectually challenging activity by either the student or the pupils. You may wish to consider subject content here and refer to Chapter 6. Suggest strategies to the student for overcoming any difficulties you have observed. With the permission of the student, discuss your observations and strategies with colleagues.

2 Draft a proforma for recording the assessment of a group of children which could be used by a student. Relate the proforma to an aspect of the programme of study for English, mathematics or science. Devise a way of indicating on the proforma where each pupil is in the three-stage model of learning we have been discussing. (In the chapter we suggested three horizontal lines, one for each stage, or three coloured dots.)

You may want to list curriculum targets on the vertical axis and children's names on the horizontal axis. The recording system should be quick to use and of the check-list variety but clear enough to inform future planning for the pupils.

Ask a student to evaluate it by using it for a week. Focus the evaluation on ease of use and usefulness for planning. Discuss the student's evaluations.

## Further reading

An excellent analysis of what happens when teachers plan, and of the relationship between intention and implementation, is Clark, C. M. and Yinger, R. J. (1987) Teacher planning, in J. Calderhead (ed.) *Exploring Teachers' Thinking*, London, Cassell.

Woods, P. (ed.) (1995) *Contemporary Issues in Teaching and Learning*, London, Routledge in association with The Open University, does not focus entirely on primary practice. However, it contains several useful papers. These include Alexander on primary practice, Brown and Campione on communities of learning and thinking for pupils in classrooms, and Patricia Murphy on the integration of learning and assessment.

Kutnick, P. and Rogers, C. (eds) (1994) *Groups in Schools*, London, Cassell, is a useful set of papers which are well grounded in research on learning and motivation in group settings.

Levine, H. (1993) Context and scaffolding in developmental studies of mother–child problem-solving dyads, in S. Chaiklin and J. Lave (eds) *Understanding Practice: Perspectives on Activity and Context*, Cambridge, CUP, unpacks the complexity of scaffolding interactions in ways which emphasize the highly interactive nature of scaffolding.

Two books on assessment published in 1994 add usefully to current understandings of assessment and pupil learning in schools and in addition place assessment within a wider policy framework. Gipps, C. (1994) *Beyond Testing: Towards a Theory*, London: Falmer, and Torrance, H. (1994) *Authentic Assessment*, Buckingham, Open University Press.

# MENTORING AND

# ASSESSING

## What is assessment? Definitions and dilemmas

At its simplest an assessment is a judgement against a criterion. From there on, discussion of assessment becomes more complex. What is the criterion? Has it been made explicit to all concerned? Is it related to expectations of average performance or to the mastery of a particular skill? What is the purpose of the assessment? Who does the assessing? Each of these questions trails in its wake implications for the work of mentors with students in their classrooms.

So far most of our discussion of mentoring has centred on ways in which mentors might support the learning of students as they move, in Lave and Wenger's terms (Lave and Wenger, 1991), towards full participation in the community of practice that is primary school teaching. We have talked about how mentors scaffold student performance both through conversations which deal with the evaluation and planning of tasks (Chapter 3) and through modelling, interventions and team-teaching (Chapter 4). Decisions about the type and level of scaffolding required by students, we have suggested, are based on assessments of student expertise and need that are made by mentors. For example, students' movement as learners through the four quadrants outlined in Figure 2.2 in Chapter 2 is directed by judgements of mentors, among others, about how well students are learning and performing.

Here we are describing the attentive *formative* assessment which is most closely related to the teacherly aspects of the role of mentors. Assessments are made in order to gather information on which decisions about a student's next learning experience may be taken. In making the formative judgements, we have just suggested, mentors are guiding students towards competent performance in a variety of areas of classroom life. Mentors' formative assessments are usually judgements that are made in order to strengthen and support student performance. In this way they fit easily with a type of mentoring that welcomes students into classrooms as 'would-be teachers' who are to develop their teaching skills in the safe environments provided by mentors.

*Summative*, or final, assessments, particularly when they are related to pass, fail or referral (the need to repeat), are much harder to undertake. This kind of assessment is always difficult, even for an external examiner who will not have established a personal and supporting mentoring relationship with a student. A lot can hang on a summative assessment. A mark for an assignment can influence a degree classification and an assessment of performance can determine the future professional life of a student.

We shall look at both formative and summative assessment in some detail later in the chapter. At this point we would like simply to identify a dilemma for mentors who are also involved in the final assessments of students, whether at an interim stage in a student's programme or at the end of the programme. The dilemma arises from the situation where the mentor is both teacherly friend and final arbiter. The situation is made more complex because all too often mentors experience a sense of personal failure when the students they have nurtured still fail to reach appropriate standards. We shall tackle the problem of the double role when we look at roles and responsibilities in assessment later in the chapter.

As we proceed with our discussion of assessment we shall emphasize, in order to diffuse some of the difficulties, the importance of having a clear assessment focus and some evidence on which to base any judgements about students. While assessment can never be an entirely neutral process in initial teacher training, because we all carry our own pictures of what is effective practice, one can attempt to make it rigorous.

We will stay with the importance of rigour a little longer. Judgement against criteria implies the use of a set of expectations which provide a focus for the act of assessment. When judgements are incorporated into a common system of assessment which aims to give parity and uniformity across assessors, we need to think about how the expectations of the assessors are standardized in some way. Here the concern is the *reliability* of the assessments. In other words, would two assessors make the same judgement on these criteria on this student?

However the situations in which student teachers learn and perform vary so much that, easy to use, standardized assessment criteria could fail to pick up the particular strengths that a student may bring to a demanding situation. Deceptively clear and simple assessment criteria may as a consequence be sacrificing *validity* for reliability. In other words the criteria may not be sensitive to what is actually going on. Issues of reliability and validity are central to any discussion of assessment and we shall return to them throughout the chapter. The idea of a community of practice in which there is continuous discussion of the criteria for effective performance will be a central theme as we examine how mentors deal with reliability and validity.

You will have noticed that we have referred consistently to criteria for the assessment of students. In initial teacher training the criteria with which you are probably most familiar are statements of competence. These will no doubt be written as sets of behaviour and capability that students are expected to demonstrate. The definitions of performance may be quite tight, but more often than not they will be presented in quite loose terms that will make considerable demands on your own professional judgement. The criteria will also probably be presented in a developmental continuum. For example, expectations of students' ability to plan for children's learning will develop over their period of study.

Assessments of performance therefore appear to be quite clearly *criterion-referenced* assessments. That is, they are based on an assessment of whether a learner can demonstrate a particular skill or show a particular capability. But there are also aspects of *norm-referenced* assessment involved in the actual act of assessment. For example, mentors' judgements will draw upon their expectations of what might normally be expected from a student teacher at a particular stage in his or her training. The more loosely the criteria are presented, the stronger will be the sense of norm referencing in the judgements of assessors as assessors try to make sense of what is expected. This is certainly not an argument for tight criteria, far from it. Rather we are recognizing and emphasizing the importance of making explicit the standards of student performance that are being used by assessors across and within schools and across programmes. Again we want to recognize the importance of the community of practice that is primary teaching, of the discussions within it and of the part that initial teacher training is playing in the community. We shall return to a discussion of competences and their specification later in the chapter where we shall draw on a study of the assessment of competences in primary classrooms carried out by the first author and Sam Twiselton (Edwards and Twiselton, 1995).

Much of what we have discussed so far will be familiar to you in the context of the assessment of pupils against the expectations of pupil performance found in the national curriculum. However, the three stages of the assessment process, that is of judging in the act of assessment, recording performance and reporting, are somewhat different when mentors are dealing with the learning of student teachers. These differences, as you would expect, stem from the nature of the relationship that exists between mentors as expert practitioners and students as 'would-be practitioners'.

If you are a mentor, while you are inducting the less expert professionals into professional practices you will need to be explicit in the way that you provide feedback on performance, yet sensitive to their beliefs that they are, like you, operating as teachers in the classroom. We have discussed contingent mentoring through, for example, team-teaching and rapid written feedback in Chapter 4. You may want to look again at the observations discussed in that chapter.

A recognition of the importance of sound feedback to students leads us on to unpack the processes of assessment recording and reporting as they are found in initial teacher training. The act of assessment itself can be broken down as follows: *listening, observing* and *judging*. The act of assessment is therefore little different from the assessment of pupils. Recording can be seen to consist largely of *noting*. It is in the area of reporting that the major distinction between the assessment of students and the assessment of pupils can be seen. Reporting, whether as interactive feedback or public summative report, has to be *honest, open* and based on *evidence*. Consequently, reporting is not always easy to manage when the objects of the report are people who see themselves in some way as colleagues while they work together with mentors in classrooms.

## Managing formative assessment

In this section we will focus on the formative assessment of teaching performance and the evaluation and planning associated with a well-orchestrated performance in a primary classroom. Although, as a mentor, you may be involved in the assessment of written work, essays and reports are rarely presented for formative assessment.

As we suggested in the first section of this chapter, formative assessment is the engine that drives well-planned active mentoring. The emphasis on active mentoring is once again important, as one alternative to it, reactive mentoring, can be a particularly limiting way to shape student behaviour and to guide them towards effective practice. In reactive mentoring formative feedback consists of corrective comments, the pointing out of errors in order to prevent their recurrence. Not only does this method of shaping behaviour do little for the relationships between students and mentors, it is neither an efficient nor an effective way of developing improved performance. Praise for achieving desired goals simply works better as a teaching principle!

We shall move on from the basic behaviourist learning theory in the final sentence of the last paragraph and now consider the model of teaching and learning we outlined in Chapter 2. There we pointed out that active mentoring was based on continuous assessment and feedback against agreed expectations of student understanding and performance. Goal setting, we suggested, is a vital aspect of student progress through the individual cycle of learning we outlined in Figure 2.2. When we discussed Figure 2.2 we emphasized the importance of quadrants B and C and the intramental learning plane in which they were placed. It is, we argued, in the intramental plane that students internalize understandings and repertoires of behaviour.

And it is when students are coping with learning in the intramental plane that formative assessment is a vital part of their assisted performance in classrooms.

In Chapter 2 we suggested that goal setting and assisted student performance could best be achieved when precise elements of performance are identified for student action. An example of an element of performance would be resourcing a group task and providing an appropriate level of language support as the children work through the task. A clear focus for student action allows greater opportunity for valid assessment of student performance against agreed aims.

Clarity of focus also makes it easier to incorporate student self-assessment into the formative assessment. Self-assessment can be valuable if students are to develop as professionals who continue to learn once they have finished their initial training. It can also be a useful basis for formative discussions with them.

We have seen self-assessment schedules for students which are directly related to areas of competence and which require students to place themselves at points on a scale linked with the competence. Some students seem to be unwilling to use these scales as, quite rightly we would argue, they do not know what the scales actually represent. What does competent performance in an area feel and look like? Others start to use the scales and then discover, as they learn more about the scope of the area of competence, that they are in fact less competent than they had originally estimated.

One way of dealing with student self-assessment that seems to work is to ask them to identify as individuals their own strengths and development needs in particular areas of competence. These assessments can then be used as the basis of discussion and the planning of future learning experiences for them. However, before students feel able to reveal their development needs they have to feel that the evidence will not be used against them at a future date. But we shall look at the conflicts inherent in the mentor assessor role a little later in this chapter.

Formative assessment can, it seems, help shape the individual learning pathway of a student and affect the pace at which it is followed. While the criteria to be used for summative assessment will provide the final goals, the interactive feedback that comes through regular discussion, and conscious highlighting, through interest and praise, of those aspects of practice that are valued, can be forces that shape a student's understandings and behaviour. The lessons about positive reinforcement we have learnt from behaviourist psychology will be familiar to teachers and managers in schools.

We have been suggesting that sound formative assessment is also dependent upon the quality of the relationships that exist between mentors and students. Formative assessment makes demands on both sets of participants. Mentors may have to suspend judgement, at least for a time, to allow students to reveal where they are in their current cycles of learning. Suspension of mentors' judgement may create minds that are open to the unexpected learning of students. It is crucial that students feel safe enough to reveal their misunderstandings; though, as we indicated earlier, when the mentor role is closely aligned with the role of final arbiter, the quality of the mentor–student relationship may be strained. The demand on students is simply that if they want to benefit from formative feedback they need to allow it to happen, to listen to what is given and act upon it in a considered fashion. When formative feedback is presented to students in written form by mentors and leads to an agenda for action, there is, of course, a record that can be traced and against which progress can be monitored.

This brings us to how to deal with the records of classroom performance that are written while students are observed in action in classrooms. Often referred to as 'crit sheets', they are produced and presented in ways that vary considerably. In reactive mentoring they may indeed live up to their title and be a critical list of faults displayed by students, together with suggestions on ways that performance might be improved. In active mentoring written feedback may be based on relatively short, but frequent, mentor observations of a previously agreed aspect of student activity. It is likely that the focus will be an area of competence that is part of the set of learning outcomes for a student at a particular stage in his or her learning.

We use the word *observation* quite deliberately. One way of assisting student performance if you are a mentor is to record some of the actions that students take, raise questions about them in your commentary and use the observations as starting points for subsequent discussions with the students. At the beginning of students' programmes you may use the evidence of your notes in order to identify areas for improvement that could take the form of action plans. The action plans could be agreed in conversations with the students after joint examination of the observations you have recorded. As the students become more competent practitioners it may be more appropriate to allow them to take the lead in identifying future actions.

Teaching is not a set of skills like tap dancing or flute playing. Rather it is the informed exercise of a complex interacting set of skills in an ever-shifting environment. Observations of student performance should place students as part of the classroom environment. Assessment of performance should identify sensitivity to and use of the teaching context. It should pick up value issues even at the level of nuance and assumption, and should take into account the quality of the relationship that students have with the children as learners. Touching on some of the matters we have just outlined can be difficult if a student is unprepared for this form of critique. A reactive mentor who, for example, questions students' assumptions about single-parent families is likely to meet more resistance than an active mentor who builds a discussion of both mentor and student assumptions into the planning process. We are not suggesting that this is easy to do. Our analysis of mentoring conversations discussed in Chapter 3 indicated that value issues were very rarely raised.

We have so far considered the content of written feedback but not the tone. How positive should you be as a mentor? The answer is that you need to be honest. If you write only positive comments but have concerns that you leave for private discussion, you are leaving yourself open to criticism and even to the formal processes of student appeal should the student finally fail or need an additional period of school experience. You can deal with any feelings of discomfort that you might have about negative comments by, as we suggested, writing your observations as a narrative of what occurred and by leading the student into consideration of the impact of alternative actions by asking specific questions.

## Managing summative assessment

A major issue here is the dilemma faced by those mentors who have to assume the role of both scaffolding guide and final judge. As we have already suggested, the combination of roles at the very least makes diagnostic assessment difficult. In addition, it is likely to encourage students to see themselves defensively as teachers rather than learners.

The problem can be overcome and is usually solved by the appointment of senior mentors who, in partnership programmes, are the main links between the universities, other mentors in other schools and mentors in their own schools. Other arrangements we have observed include a pairing of mentors so that Mentor A mentors his or her students and makes final assessments on the students of Mentor B and *vice-versa*. The first model emphasizes reliability both within and across schools. The second model may be more sensitive to issues of validity of assessment, as the paired mentor is more likely to have a better knowledge of the strengths and weaknesses of the students involved. Both models are based on the development of a set of shared understandings of what is appropriate performance at a particular stage in the students' programme of learning. Both models demand a great deal from the professional judgement of the assessors.

A study by Edwards and Twiselton of how teachers assessed the competence of classroom assistants who were trained and assessed in their classrooms threw into relief problems of professional judgements and teachers' concerns in relation to the expectations held of them (Edwards and Twiselton, 1995). The teachers involved in assessing the student classroom assistants were told by the university and by the local education authority, which had an interest in the training programme, that members of both bodies were relying on the professional judgement of the teachers to ensure the reliability and validity of the assessments they made of student performance. It was argued that the exercise of that judgement would be individually empowering for the teachers concerned.

That was not how the teachers saw it. They reported their unease about the reliability of their individual judgements. Indeed they felt that their professionalism was put under threat as they had no confidence in their individual ability to assess the students with any reliability. They also had considerable concerns about the reliability of the standards across the training programme. The response of the teachers was fascinating. They engaged in what could only be termed 'intelligent resistance'. They assessed the students, but not on the criteria they were given by the university. They instead used their own judgements on student performance that were often not in any way related to the aims and intended learning outcomes of the programme. In fact they used their professional judgement but did not align it to the demands of the programme of study of the students. Their assessments were as a consequence invalid in the terms of the programme.

The teachers also saw a more positive solution to the dilemmas they faced when they dealt with their own doubts about common standards. They eventually requested regular meetings of mentors so that understanding of standards could be shared and as a result their confidence in the reliability and validity of standards developed. We return once again to the work of Jean Lave (Lave and Wenger, 1991; Chaiklin and Lave, 1993). Understandings of the knowledge base that is held in the community of practice that is primary education may become explicit and be developed in discussion of that practice by participants in the community.

But, as the teachers in the study we have just discussed noted, discussion of standards of performance need to be set against criteria that are set for the performance of students. When we look at the classroom performance of students, the criteria are in the form of statements of competence. In addition there is usually a developmental aspect to the statements of competence. The most commonly used framework for understanding the development of competence in professional education is the model produced by Dreyfus and Dreyfus (1986). What follows is a summary of their model of professional skills acquisition.

*Level 1: novice*
- Rigidly keeps to taught rules and agreed plans
- Has little sensitivity to the intricacies of the situation
- Has no discretionary judgement.

*Level 2: advanced beginner*
- Follows guidelines for action based on attributes or aspects of situations which are global in nature and recognizable only after prior experience
- Has fairly limited awareness of the complexities of professional situations
- Cannot distinguish with ease between the relative importance of attributes and aspects of situations.

*Level 3: competent*
- Can cope with busy situations with competing demands
- Can consider actions in relation to longer-term goals
- Engages in considered and informed planning
- Uses standardized and routine procedures.

*Level 4: proficient*
- Perceives situations holistically
- Can discern what is important in a situation
- Recognizes differences from normal patterns
- Decisions involve less effort
- Can adapt basic guidelines to fit the needs of specific situations.

*Level 5: expert*
- Is no longer dependent on specific rules and guidelines
- Can call on intuition and tacitly held understandings for directing actions
- Is analytic in new situations only
- Possesses a view of what is possible.

While this model provides a useful framework for understanding the development of practical competence, it pays little attention to the learning that lies behind the demonstration of competence. It can be seen as a model of self-perpetuating notions of professional competence. As Eraut (1994) argues, it underestimates the problem of expert fallibility. Throughout this text we have been suggesting that there is more to teaching than performance in a classroom and that what is important is informed practice that can adapt and develop to meet changing requirements. Nevertheless the Dreyfus and Dreyfus model is a useful one, not least because it allows a strong connection to be made between pre-service training and continuing professional learning.

Let us pursue the developmental perspective. For students on a first teaching practice, who might be expected to be at Level 2, competences to be demonstrated might include the following.

- An ability to vary the management of pupil learning.
- An ability to use questioning to engage children's learning.
- An ability to provide resources that support children's learning.

By the time the student reaches the final stages of a training programme and is at Level 3, the statements may include these.

- An ability to manage the learning of a whole class.
- An ability to plan teaching sessions for the learning of children across the ability range.
- An ability to work effectively with other teachers in long-term curriculum planning.

These appear relatively loose statements of behaviour which may not take into account the varying demands of the situations in which they might be brought into play. As one extremely experienced primary school teacher asked us, 'How can I be sure that I am right when I assess my students?' As researchers, our reply is that you can gather evidence. The evidence may be used in discussions with students, but in the end evidence has to be the basis on which you make decisions about students.

The act of assessment is not so much a question of, as one of the assessors in the Edwards and Twiselton study put it, 'watching a student and looking for a competence'. Competence is more a matter of general capability observed over time and in different situations. But sound assessment will require observation. An extract from an interview with a teacher who was involved in the teaching assistant study illustrates the point. She is talking about the difficulties involved in assessing the competence of trainees while working in a busy classroom and is describing how she managed one assessment.

> She was doing this sorting activity, going through the motions without understanding it at all. The children were sorting the toys in a completely confused way and she didn't even realise. When I looked at what she had written about the activity the problems weren't mentioned. I could easily have signed it (the competence record) if I hadn't happened to have seen her.
>
> (Edwards and Twiselton, 1995)

The lesson learnt from the teaching assistant study was that time for the assessment process needs to be created for mentors.

In addition to the assessment of teaching competence, if you are a mentor, you may find that you are required to assess students' written work. Marking may be on a pass/fail basis or you might have to use a complex marking scale with specific criteria. In any case you will need to be aware of the assessment criteria that are being used. A good starting point is the Definitive Course Document (DCD) of the programme of study. You may well be provided with extracts from it in the documentation you receive from your partner university if you are in a partnership scheme. If you are not working directly with a university the documentation should be held in its complete form in your school. The DCD will give the flavour of the programme. It will provide information on the purposes of assignments and should, for example in a degree programme, give some indication of what, say, an assignment meriting a 2.i or a 2.ii grading might look like in general terms. For example, a 2.i assignment will demonstrate engagement with the question in ways that demonstrate an informed analytic response that is tightly argued. A 2.ii assignment will show direct engagement with the question in a sound and informed manner.

However each assignment will be designed to make sure that students have the opportunity to demonstrate the learning outcomes that are related to a particular aspect of their programme. As a result certain features of the assignment may need to be highlighted in the assessment criteria that are used. For example, students may be required to show their ability to learn from their experiences in the classroom. In this case the assessment criteria would refer to self-awareness and the use of classroom examples.

Some universities use marking grids to help guide the assessment of specific assignments. These can be helpful and particularly so if they are

*Table 8.1*    Marking grid

| Grade | Use of literature | Design | Analysis | Presentation |
|-------|-------------------|--------|----------|--------------|
| A | Informed syntheses of relevant literature | Design allows the sensitive exploration of the research question | Rigorous and detailed, substantiates assertions | Lucid and relevant |
| B | Referred to relevant studies | Research question is clear and followed through | Aware of the limitations of the study | Clearly argued, well organized |

C and so on

used as starting points for a sharing of understanding of the standards expected from students between markers. A marking grid for a school-based research project may look like Table 8.1. (We have not given full details under each heading.)

If you are not provided with a marking grid it may be useful to work with colleagues to create something like this, as grids certainly provide an opportunity to discuss what is actually meant by the bland statements that are often used when we assess. One decision you may want to make is the relative weighting of each of the columns in the grid. In the research project example we have just given, is presentation as important as analysis? Students also need to know what weighting is to be given. Grids of this type are also useful when you moderate the marks when all the assignments have been marked.

## The implications of the assessor role for classroom management

The assessment of students is clearly potentially as time-consuming as the assessment of pupils and, like the assessment of pupils, it is best incorporated into normal classroom practices that have learning as a priority. We have emphasized the importance of evidence and particularly observational evidence when assessing student progress. Our suggestions have implications for how students are allowed to operate in classrooms and how mentors use their time.

Our observational data and our analyses of mentoring conversations showed us that the majority of the mentors in the programme we monitored gave students exactly what the students wanted. That is, they provided safe places in which students could *be* teachers and they confirmed the students' sense of themselves as teachers by teaching other groups of children or by leaving the classroom entirely. We had very few examples in our observational data of teachers who observed students and regularly used the observations as the basis of discussion. We discussed the strategies of mentors who observed in this way in Chapter 4.

Of course, in the programme we monitored, the required number of observations were made by the teachers who were ultimately responsible for the summative assessment of the students. But we have also have been suggesting that observation should be used as the basis of formative assessment too. Were observations to become more centrally part of the mentor role, there would be implications for how mentor time is used when students are teaching. For example, it may be appropriate for mentors to set pupil tasks that require only light teacher monitoring at times when students are observed while they teach. The management of time in classrooms when the teaching role has been extended to include the teaching of student teachers is quite a challenge and may be picked up when we consider action research and the development of mentor practice in the next chapter.

## Activities

1 Read several of the most recent 'crit' sheets you have written for students. What appear to be your major preoccupations in them? If you are mentor to more than one student compare your comments on each student. Do you comment on the same topics in both cases? Do you talk about pupil learning and classroom management? Does your feedback give suggestions for future development of the student? Compare your feedback and your analysis of it with at least one colleague. If at all possible, both of you observe the same students. What are the similarities and differences in content and style in your feedback? Can any differences be justified? Together identify some topics for particular focus next time you observe these students.

2 Bring a record of student competence that is at least partially completed to a meeting with fellow mentors who will arrive similarly prepared. Discuss the criteria you each used as you decided on the degree of competence demonstrated by the students. Think back to when you assessed and list the criteria you used. Compare your criteria with those used by your colleagues. Then compare your criteria with the descriptors provided by Dreyfus and Dreyfus and presented in this chapter.

## Further reading

Proctor, A., Entwistle, M., Judge, B. and Mckenzie-Murdoch, S. (1995) *Learning to Teach in the Primary Classroom*, London, Routledge, is written for student teachers. However it provides schedules for classroom observations and student self-assessment criteria which could be used by mentors as they assess student performance.

Yeomans, R. and Sampson, J. (eds) (1995) *Mentoring in the Primary School*, London, Falmer, explores mentorship across three types of initial training programme: PGCE, B.Ed and an articled teacher scheme. Case studies of mentors are analysed. The role of mentors as assessors of students and the implications of this for mentors' relationships with trainees are usefully addressed.

Eraut, M. (1994) *Developing Professional Knowledge and Competence*, London, Falmer, is a finely considered analysis of competences and professional development. Though it focuses to a large extent on teacher training, it places teacher education in a wider set of competence-based professional training initiatives and considers the implications for professional learning.

Wolf, A. (1995) *Competence-Based Assessment*, Buckingham, Open University Press, reviews the origins of competence-based assessment and gives an informed perspective on current critiques of the assessment of competence and the potential that their assessment might have for professional training.

Edwards, A. and Knight, P. (eds) (1995) *Assessing Competence in Higher Education*, London, Kogan Page, contains some interesting papers. These include Hustler on recording achievement, Tomlinson and Saunders on competence profiling in teacher training and Winter on the assessment of professional competences (the ASSET programme).

# SECTION III

# MENTORS AS
# RESEARCHERS

## What do we mean by research?

Research in schools and classrooms has no mystery to it. It is simply a process of systematic enquiry into an area of activity on which one collects the best quality evidence one can. But let us just unpack that definition and look in turn at *systematic, activity* and *evidence*. We shall do that by first of all recognizing that what mentors are doing is practitioner research and that practitioner research is the practice of the possible.

### Systematic enquiry

Systematic enquiry can be a complex affair and is crucial to the quality of professional research. Mentors are, however, first of all professional teachers who are already dealing with an extension to their teaching roles when they mentor student teachers. Being a practitioner researcher has to take second place. Hopefully nevertheless you will become convinced by our argument that practitioner research can support practice. Systematic enquiry, if it is to support mentor practice, therefore has to fit in with classroom practice. Practitioner enquiry can be as simple as keeping a coherent focus to professional curiosity about aspects of practice and using ways of gathering evidence about practice which are true to the focus of that curiosity.

### A focus on teaching and learning activities

The activities that are the focuses of mentors' attention as practitioner researchers do need to be defined at some point. But most enquiries start fairly wide and narrow down. If you are a mentor, one activity might be an examination of what you and your colleagues write in the formal feedback you give to students. The enquiry may not have started with that focus, but may have taken a more general starting point such as feedback to students and then narrowed down in focus after initial observations and perhaps discussions with colleagues.

### Gathering good quality evidence

The evidence that is gathered, as the focus activity is examined, does need to be of sufficiently good quality to allow discussion of it with colleagues. Above all it needs to be of good enough quality to allow the consideration of further actions on the basis of it, regardless of whether these are research or mentoring actions. However, although we are stressing the quality of the evidence that is gathered, it is important that the methods used to collect the evidence do not disrupt classroom life. We shall be looking at *nonintrusive research methods* later in the chapter. At this point we shall simply stress the need to gather the best quality evidence you can, but shall also recognize that mentors' priorities in the classroom are the children and their learning.

## Researching with others

There are already some assumptions in what we have written about the kind of research you might be doing as a mentor. First of all we have assumed that your research would take your work as a mentor as a focus. In fact it may not directly do that. If you are working with students who are so able that they require little active mentoring, you may find that they are ready to work with you as co-enquirers into particular aspects of, for example, children's learning or classroom management. Indeed it may also be appropriate for you to work in this way with less competent students as they undertake systematic enquiries as part of their own programmes of study.

Another assumption we have made is that you will be working with colleagues, or that at least you will have someone else with whom you can discuss what you have seen and how you are interpreting it. Given all we have said about the importance of discussion, it will come as no surprise that we suggest that someone to talk to is a valuable resource. The extract that follows comes from an American teacher who was involved with a group of teachers from a number of schools in taking a researcherly approach to a curriculum development project. It gives you some sense of what can be gained from sharing the teacher-researcher experience with others.

This group breaks down the isolation for me. I feel as though I am now part of a bigger picture. This gives me a chance to talk and to think. I feel so much more confident as a teacher, as I realize that a lot of my frustration isn't all my fault. I share more readily, and am not so resistant to others' ideas. . . . What this group has done for me is help me to know that I have something to say, that questions are something to say. . . . I feel that this group is a bridge, letting me go back and forth from myself and this group to my larger worlds and then back again.

(Miller, 1990: 115)

This teacher's discussion of her personal confidence, her finding a voice and her use of the conversations as a bridge from her own private world to the semi-private world of the group to larger worlds, are all important. All are evidence of the gains available for practitioner researchers who are in a position to collaborate or at least to discuss their classroom evidence.

## How to use this chapter

Arguably this chapter could have been the first chapter in the book. In Chapter 1 we introduced a simple evaluation cycle, and suggested there that mentors start to keep a reflective diary as a way of recording and developing their practice as a mentor. We have also emphasized throughout the book that although we are offering ideas that have come from our own study of mentoring, the ideas are open to the scrutiny and critique of practitioners. The most important research for individual mentors and their colleagues is the research that provides insights into their schools, classrooms and students. Our research is simply a starting point for mentors' enquiries. Mentors may want to pick up some of the questions we have raised and test them in their workplaces. Readers may want to try some of the data collection methods we have used and mentioned elsewhere in the book. But above all we want to emphasize that practitioner research is an important part of the process of developing practice.

We are being highly selective in the types of research that we suggest are useful for practitioner researchers. Our selection is based entirely on our recognition that practitioners are usually working in one setting and that any research that is done must be relevant to practice as teachers and mentors. The two types of research we propose are *case study research* and *action research*. The first allows practitioners to raise important questions and to look in fresh ways at familiar scenes. The second often builds on case study to tackle ways of developing practice.

## Case study research

First of all we need to consider what is the case to be studied. One simple definition is that a case is an event or person or people or place which

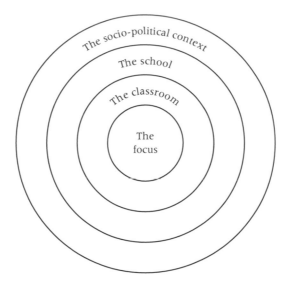

*Figure 9.1*   Connecting case to context

can be studied systematically over time so that one can build up a picture of the focus of the case in the context in which it occurs. A useful way of visualizing a case and its place in the wider context of education is to see a set of concentric circles at the centre of which is the case to be examined (see Figure 9.1). If the case is, for example, a group of children when they work at mathematics tasks over two weeks, the focus of your gaze as researcher will be the children. But at the same time you will build up a picture of how the children interact with other children, how they use space, time and materials, how they interact with you and the student you are mentoring. The topics we have just listed will raise a lot of questions about general classroom practices. But they may also alert you to whole-school issues, for example timetabling or subject-specialist teaching. These school-based topics, in turn, take you out into wider educational debate of a quite fundamental nature.

In classroom research there is a lot of scope for defining the case that sits at the core of the concentric circles shown in Figure 9.1. A case might be, for example, a group of children, an area in the classroom, a time of day, a particular teaching technique or a resource. Case study demands that you focus your gaze on what goes on in the case and allows you to use your observations to refine progressively the focus of your attention. Case study research is extremely useful because it answers the question 'What is going on here?' It does so in ways that let you look at the detail of the case in much of its messy complexity. At the same time it ensures that you pick up at least a little on the context in which the case is operating.

A case study generally takes a fairly clear focus and often progressively narrows the focus as evidence is gathered and considered. The quality of the evidence you gather is therefore important because the continuous refining of the precise focus of a case study is often driven by the data that you have already collected and considered. Case studies as a consequence need to be constructed with the best quality data you can muster.

Even so, case studies based on the richest of data are often criticized on a number of counts. First of all it is said that a case study cannot tell the world about anything more than a set of experiences in one context. The analysis of a single case, it is argued, can have no general use. In order to be able to generalize your findings and claim that they may be more widely applicable, for example in other schools, you need to work with large samples and not single cases. This criticism can be countered in two ways.

Firstly, a single case study is not always carried out with the intention of generalizing, but with the intention of finding out more about what is going on in a particular setting so that further questions can be raised. The further questions may be related directly to practice and lead to an action research study. But we will return to action research later in this chapter. Single case studies may also indicate areas where a more extensive study, perhaps a survey study, would be useful.

Another powerful way of countering the criticism that generalizations cannot be made from a case study is to organize a comparative analysis of several cases. The comparison of cases can work well when several practitioner researchers are working in a similar area and take the same focus of enquiry but in different settings. The cases can be held alongside each other and similarities and differences explored. Common themes of experience can be extracted as the cases are compared. Groups of Key Stage 1 teachers who examined the impact of Standard Assessment Tasks (SATs) on their classroom practices worked in this way and locally built up convincing pictures of the disruption caused by testing which were fed to policy makers.

Another major criticism of case study research is that it lacks rigour and depends on the individual bias of the person who is compiling the study. One way of dealing with this as an individual researcher is to use more than one way of collecting evidence. We talked about validity and reliability in relation to assessment in Chapter 8. Validity and reliability are also concerns in case study research. In other words case study researchers need to feel as assured as they can be that they have got a sound purchase on the events they are observing. To feel some confidence in the reliability and validity of the picture being compiled, case study researchers need to get several perspectives on the case. In research terms this may involve taking observation as a primary method for collecting evidence and backing this up with records of student or children's progress and perhaps a research diary commentary (see Chapter 1) that might include conversations with other colleagues.

The case that is built up will be based on rich data. It may threaten to take up a great deal of time. Because of this we strongly recommend that limits are placed on case study research undertaken by practitioners. This can be done by taking a narrow focus as soon as possible and by setting a short time limit. Cases can then be used, as we have already outlined, to build up a wider data-base alongside those of other practitioners. The larger group of cases may then be used to influence the policies that, for example, direct practice in schools and universities. Alternatively a single case can be used as a starting point for another form of enquiry, action research; and it is to this that we now turn.

## Action research

In Chapter 1 we discussed a framework through which mentors might engage with their own learning as mentors. The framework was a straightforward evaluation cycle which started with a review of the current situation, identified goals, suggested the selection of strategies for achieving the goals and emphasized the importance of performance indicators as evidence of having achieved the goals that had been identified. We now want to consider how that simple evaluation model may be developed into a framework for systematic development of practice through action research.

Let us start by trying to define action research. The evaluation cycle we have just outlined is a good beginning. However there are several crucial features to action research that distinguish it from evaluation. First of all the focus of action research is the evaluation of one's own practice. Secondly, the evaluation is based on the careful examination of evidence that is gathered on that practice. Ideally that examination is carried out in conversation with at least one other person so that fresh perspectives can be brought to bear on the evidence and your own interpretations of it. Thirdly, action research draws on evidence available in the public domain when deciding on plans and strategies. The public domain may be represented by the work of other mentors in other schools or by published research.

Figure 9.2 shows a cycle of action research which starts with *review*, moves to *plan* and then to *act* and *monitor* and finally again to *review* before proceeding once more to *replan* and a continuation of the cycle. The best way of getting to grips with action research is, however, not to grapple with models provided by other people but to do it. The second best way is to look at how other practitioners have carried out action research.

If we look at Figure 9.2 we recognize that the first stage of initial review is a crucially important element in the cycle. Many action research studies start with a small case study which is based on an exploration of practice in context and which allows an examination of material available in the published literature and in the work of other practitioners. If the case study does what is expected of it, it should raise questions about practice that can be followed up as practice is developed and its development is monitored through action research.

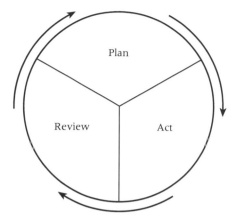

*Figure 9.2* An action research cycle

If you are a mentor the best starting point for an initial review may be observation of what is going on in your own classroom. If you were to stand still for no more than two minutes and watch an activity in which you are already interested or about which you have some concern, you may find it a fruitful exercise. In Chapter 1 we introduced the idea of a reflective diary. The left-hand pages can be used for a series of notes about what has been observed and the right-hand page for a later commentary on the observations in which you begin to raise questions about the possibilities for the development of practice.

The planning stage will draw on these observations and strategies will be devised. You may, for example, decide to try out the contingent mentoring we described in Chapter 4 as a way of shaping the practice of a student who seems to require guidance once she starts to work with children. It is important that desired outcomes are decided at this stage. For example you may want to ensure that the student learns to use specific techniques for keeping the attention of a small group while she introduces an activity. By identifying such performance indicators you are not limiting the outcomes of the development of practice, but you are providing some benchmarks against which you can consider your actions and their impact on the students. Often a great deal can be learnt when performance indicators are not achieved. There may have been problems inherent in the mentoring situation, or the indicators themselves may have been inappropriate and your expectations unreasonable.

The action stage is always a demanding one. It requires that teacher-mentors who are researching their own practice operate at two levels. They have to act and they have to monitor their actions and the impact of those actions on the student teachers and on the children. The monitoring therefore has to be manageable and not intrusive. Once again the reflective diary is useful. Jottings in the diary, as and when it is possible to make them, can be expanded or simply used as the basis of discussion with a colleague. Other ways of gathering evidence on the impact of practice include children's work, students' plans and evaluations, tape-recordings (see Chapter 3), and photographs. The latter are particularly powerful as they can so easily be used as the basis of discussion at the evaluation stage.

After completion of the action stage, the evidence that has been collected should be set against the performance indicators that were identified at the planning stage. In other words, practitioners sit down with someone and discuss their evidence. The discussion will consider not only the outcomes, for example the quality of the students' planning for children's learning in mathematics, but also the processes that might impact on their planning. Processes might include the fact that students are bussed to school with the consequence that there is insufficient time to evaluate and plan with their mentors. Evidence of this kind is therefore extremely useful in creating a case for the improvement of provision.

Group action research is therefore likely to be still more powerful. We have already stressed the value of talking about evidence and practice with colleagues. We have also suggested that a number of case studies that tell the same story can be influential. The same can be said of group action research. Action research is particularly useful because it can be incorporated into school quality assurance systems. We shall discuss this further in Chapter 11.

Group action research can also be a useful staff development strategy. Let us consider the experience of Janet who was a senior mentor in a primary school. She received mentor training at the university with which her school was partnered. Part of the deal with the university was that she would provide some training and guidance to the other teachers in the school who would be working on a day-to-day basis with the student teachers who were placed in the school. Janet was well aware that there was a lot more to mentoring than letting the students use the children and classroom resources while they learnt to teach by trial and error. She also knew that under the revised training arrangements the university would not be able to give the support to classteachers that it had provided in the past. On top of this she knew that mentoring was not a priority activity for some of her colleagues who had yet to feel the impact of the revised arrangements with the university. As senior mentor it was Janet's responsibility to ensure that the students received a sound training while they were placed in the school. She had to do something to get her colleagues to think and talk about their work as mentors.

She decided to take an action research approach to the development of mentor practice amongst her colleagues. A summary of the actions taken by Janet gives some feel for the potential within group action research for the sharing of understandings and the shaping of the practice of mentoring. Janet decided to take as her first focus the extent to which students were pushed in at the deep end of practice and were asked to teach almost as soon as they arrived in the school. Influenced by the work of Lave and Wenger (1991) which we discussed in Chapter 2, she decided to explore the potential for what Lave and Wenger describe as the *legitimate peripheral participation* of student teachers in the community of practice that operates in a school.

### Stage 1: Review

Janet called a meeting of the colleagues who would be mentors just before a group of students arrived in school to start a school experience placement. She talked are her own concerns over her own practice as a mentor and her own propensity to allow students to rush into teaching. She described some of the ideas that had come from her own reading of Lave and Wenger and said that she was going to be a lot more cautious about getting students to teach at the start of the next placement. She asked her colleagues whether they saw any merit in what she was saying and whether they would be willing to try to do the same. There was some hesitation and it was agreed that the best way forward would be to monitor how students coped with the first few days of their time in school. The mentors agreed to meet at the end of the first week of the students' practice with some observations of how the students were coping.

### Stage 2: Planning

At the next meeting the mentors shared their observations. They discussed what they had seen the students do. A common theme was the extent to which the students appeared to be coping on their own with specific tasks but were frequently having difficulties with the need to attend relentlessly to matters of general classroom discipline. Janet suggested that they tried a sequence of actions and evaluated how it worked. The sequence was to ask the students to watch their mentors over one day as they dealt continuously with the minutiae of classroom order and to require them to keep a written record of the actions they observed and their impact. The written record would then be used as a starting point for a conversation between each student and his or her mentor at the end of the day. It was agreed that all the mentors would try this and would themselves keep notes on how it worked so that they could evaluate the actual mentoring strategy when they next met as a group.

### Stage 3: Action and monitoring

All the mentors tried the sequence to a greater or lesser degree. Monitoring was largely a few notes made at the end of the day and some comments from the students.

*Stage 4: Review*

The discussion between the mentors started with how they felt about being watched. It soon progressed to an examination of the value of being able to talk in a positive way to students about discipline instead of simply correcting their errors and undermining their control by stepping in and taking over when things went wrong. They also touched on how the students felt about not always teaching but sometimes doing nothing but watching. And they shared the ways in which they managed the end-of-day discussions with students. This took the group to its next focus which was the purpose and management of mentoring conversations. A second action research cycle was started.

In the four stages we have just outlined, the power of group action research for the learning and developing expertise of participants is quite clear. At the same time action research allowed Janet to get the kind of practice she felt would work to the benefit of students, into the repertoire of her colleagues. Had her colleagues not been pleased with the outcomes they would not have adopted that particular practice. Nevertheless the ensuing discussions about student learning and the mentors' understandings of the processes of mentoring would no doubt still have been of value in developing a sense amongst her colleagues of what mentoring might entail.

## Research as co-enquiry with students

Joint enquiry into aspects of practice alongside the students who are learning to teach in the classroom often seemed to us some kind of Holy Grail we would never find in the data we collected. It has maintained that status. Yet collaboration between mentors and students in enquiry into dilemmas that teachers face in their practice would seem to have some value. One example of a complex dilemma may be how to achieve a balance in allowing pupils access to some activities based on friendship groups and some based on differentiated tasks. Less demanding dilemmas might be how to make parents feel welcome in the classroom without allowing them to disrupt the first ten minutes of the day, or how to encourage girls to work skilfully with construction toys. Conversations between mentors and students as these dilemmas are explored would seem to have enormous potential (Edwards, 1996).

Because we are seeing mentoring as a process of induction of beginning teachers into participation in the community of practice of primary school teaching, we have emphasized dialogues around practice as a key feature of that induction. We have made no mention of, for example, the application of theory to practice, as for us the idea is a non-starter. So how is teacher knowledge about teaching passed on to students? We have indicated in Chapter 3 that planning and evaluation conversations that focus on how students set tasks for children are often no more than vehicles for ensuring that tasks are implemented smoothly. Is perhaps a focus on dilemmas another way of enabling teacher-mentors to make explicit their understandings about the principles of teaching and learning in primary classrooms? The definition of the expert practitioner given by Dreyfus and Dreyfus (1986) in Chapter 8 would suggest that it is.

Carter (1992) suggests that current beliefs about teacher knowledge allow us to see teacher knowledge as 'practical and "contextualised" in the sense that it is knowledge of common dilemmas teachers face in classroom life' (p. 110). She goes on to argue that when teachers face these dilemmas they develop 'practical arguments' which are a form of knowledge about teaching. Given the difficulties involved in making teacher knowledge explicit that were identified in Chapter 3, the examination of dilemmas may open up possibilities for an analysis of practice.

Russell and Munby (1991) go a little further in their discussion of what they call 'puzzles' in teaching. Like Carter, they are here drawing on their experience of work and research with experienced teachers. They argue that puzzles or dilemmas stimulate the reframing of teacher understanding which in turn 'mediates between theory and practice, revealing new meanings in theory and new strategies for practice' (p. 166). For Russell and Munby, puzzles therefore provide an opportunity to examine the familiar afresh. They argue that teachers develop their own professional knowledge by working with those puzzles in their own practice. Like us they are unhappy with notions of the application of theory to practice and they too dislike the metaphor of 'dissemination' of ideas. As we have argued throughout this book, one particularly powerful way of undermining the separation of theory from practice that is implied in the use of the words 'dissemination' and 'application' is to see both theory and practice as involved in mutually constructing understandings of practice as part of developing a community of practice of primary education.

Dealing with dilemmas and puzzles in collaboration with student teachers may have some advantages for all concerned. Identifying a dilemma and the strategies to deal with it would seem to provide some opportunity for aspects of teacher professional knowledge and particularly knowledge about teaching, to be made explicit and available to students for their consideration. At the same time, according to Russell and Munby, dealing with puzzles in ways that demand that problems be opened up and discussed with others as problematic does stimulate the development of professional knowledge in experienced teachers.

Yet we know that student teachers are reluctant to engage with the riskiness of identifying problems and tackling them. In addition, in our data at least, students revealed some unwillingness to explore the perspectives that mentors held on their own practice. It is unsurprising, therefore, that we found no evidence of co-enquiry of this kind in our data. What we are suggesting is that it might be possible to develop the practice of mentoring to include this activity, at least with newly qualified teachers and with students who appear ready for some challenge in their teaching. It may be something that could be explored as a staff group and its feasibility tested as a piece of mentor research.

## Activities

We are not suggesting specific activities as a follow-up to reading this section of the book. Both case study research and action research require a focus that has meaning for the researcher. Our expectation therefore is that these approaches to enquiry will be used as you explore aspects of practice and schooling that are considered elsewhere in the book.

Nevertheless we would like to emphasize strongly the use of a reflective research diary of the kind that we outlined in Chapter 1. It allows one to base the development of practice on evidence and can be the starting point for the professional development conversations with colleagues or students that we have been advocating.

## Further reading

There are a large number of 'how to do research' texts available. A comprehensive yet basic text on action research is Hopkins, D. (1993) *A Teacher's Guide to Classroom Research*, 2nd edn, Buckingham, Open University Press. Edwards, A. and Talbot, R. (1994) *The Hard-Pressed Researcher*, London, Longman, is directed at practitioner researchers. It covers case study research and action research as well as surveys and other research designs, their associated data collection methods and how to write about research.

Bassey, M. (1995) *Creating Education Through Research*, Kirklington, Kirklington Moor Press/BERA, is a highly readable yet challenging perspective on the relationships that can exist between research and education. It is aimed at both the beginning researcher, in the detail on process it provides, and at the more expert, in the questions it raises about the nature and purposes of research in education. It is available from BERA, 15 St John's Street, Edinburgh.

Nias, J. and Groundwater-Smith, S. (eds) (1988) *The Enquiring Teacher: Supporting and Sustaining Teacher Research*, London, Falmer, is a collection of papers by teacher-researchers and higher education tutors who are committed to the development of provision through the support of teacher research. It demonstrates what teacher research can achieve and faces many of the difficulties involved.

This list does not reflect the diversity and extent of the papers on teacher research and by teachers on their research. However, we want to encourage you to do your own research and to think about making it more publicly available through, for example, workshops, conference presentations and publications.

# MENTORING AND SCHOOL DEVELOPMENT

## School-based teacher training: just another initiative?

Michael Fullan in his examination of the forces of change afoot within and around schools comes up with a diagnosis of a disease suffered in a large number of schools (Fullan, 1993). The disease is *projectitis*. Its symptoms can be observed when the latest innovation is taken on by a school without much consideration of the implications of the additional activity. The question that has to be asked is whether school-based teacher training, in whatever shape it operates, is simply another project that is added on to the activities of a school. An important supplementary question is then whether involvement in initial training can be integrated into current priorities and activities in a school. Perhaps even more pertinent is whether the development of schools is actually enhanced by increasing their involvement in initial training?

This set of questions can be placed alongside another set of concerns, this time originating from analyses of student need. Goodlad (1990), writing like Fullan from a North American perspective, argues that the usual system of placing a trainee teacher in a single classroom with one cooperating teacher is 'a seriously flawed approach'. As an alternative he encourages us to 'expand our thinking' and to examine how schools and universities might together create schools in which exemplary practice occurs.

Goodlad's ideas are evident in the creation of Professional Development

Schools (PDS) in North America in the early 1990s. PDS are based on the idea that schools evolve as centres of excellence as a result of collaboration over time between schools and departments of education in universities (Holmes Group, 1990). Evaluation of these developments is still quite patchy and we are not attempting to propose a dive into development schools. Rather we want to look at the implications of a whole-school approach to initial teacher training. We shall focus on partnerships with higher education in the next chapter. Here we want to take the schools' perspectives, and examine how schools might respond as organizations to the integration of initial teacher training into their priorities and practices.

Expanding our thinking about initial training in schools also means that we need to think of students as only one of several sets of learners in a school. In addition to the pupils, other learners will include teachers, support staff and sometimes parents. The idea of *the learning school* is by now a familiar one (Elliott, 1991; Fullan, 1991). Mentoring is provided for newly qualified teachers, and in-house staff development, often offered by subject leaders, is universal.

The idea of a learning school fits well with the ideas of Lave and Wenger (1991) that we have been pursuing throughout this book. Their view of a developing community of practice in which ideas are tested and contested and meanings negotiated in dialogues about practice, can be translated into the picture of an organization in which development is based on the increased professional understanding of the individuals who work within it. Their notion that practitioners can take up positions within the community of practice is also helpful, as it enables us to see that qualified teachers might move slowly from peripheral participation in, for example, the integration of information technology in their classrooms to eventual central participation in integrative practices, once confidence and competence is gained. It also, as we have already argued, allows us to see that higher education-based practitioners are part of the community of practice.

The role of mentors, whether they are working with students in training, with beginning teachers or with their colleagues as subject leaders, is obviously an important one. We would argue, however, that mentoring is an activity which has yet to achieve its potential in schools. Part of that potential is that mentors could be seen as important agents of change in schools. But for that to happen, schools need to recognize that the potential exists.

## The mentor role

Being a mentor involves taking on a new set of functions and perhaps thinking differently about your professional role. Whenever a role is taken on, both our own expectations of what it might involve and the expectations of others can shape the role. These expectations can in turn have an impact on our sense of who we are and what we can do. We are moving here to an exploration of *mentor identity*. The idea of identity is often useful when examining the creation of new roles. Our sense of identity or who we are has been described as an 'organising principle for action' (Harré, 1983). This line suggests that a strong sense of being a mentor would impact on a large number of the professional decisions one might make when involved with pupils and colleagues as well as with students.

If you are a mentor in an initial training programme, does the role feel to you different in any way from being a teacher who has students in his or her classroom for a period of school experience? Do you see mentoring students as an exciting new role? You may feel, for example, that being a mentor is now an important and well-integrated part of your professional identity. On the other hand you may feel that your mentor role is only one of many roles that you have in school and, indeed, were you to have to make a priority list of these roles, you would not place being a mentor very near the top of the list. You might feel that being a mentor is an exhilarating addition to your idea of what being a teacher involves. Therefore you would like to be able to make more of the opportunities you believe it presents to the school and to integrate it more firmly into your own professional identity.

We found examples of all these views of what being a mentor was like in our study of mentoring in primary schools. The responses told us quite a bit about the opportunities for professional development as a mentor in the schools we visited. Some schools were more able than others to allow the emergence of new roles and functions. These enabling schools appeared to be schools which had structures that encouraged the wide-ranging professional development of the teachers who worked there.

Being a mentor, if it involves active mentoring, is clearly a new role which needs to be accommodated into the dynamics of a developing school. If it is not recognized by the school as an important new role and taken seriously as a part of the dynamics of the school, there is the danger that mentors will be *desert-islanded* with their students in ways we outlined in Chapter 1. One consequence of desert-islanding is that students and mentors are disconnected from the rest of the school. While it is clear that the isolation of mentor and student that would result from desert-islanding would not be to the advantage of the students, we shall also argue that it presents a missed opportunity for primary schools.

Mentoring, then, if taken seriously, is an additional function which has to be incorporated into the priorities and practices of school and needs to fit into existing patterns of relationships and responsibilities. There is frequently some resistance from members of communities when new roles are created and inserted into existing patterns. Role theory tells us that new roles can be incorporated and the resulting adjustments made by a community when it values the new role. The potential value to schools of mentoring in initial training will be one theme in this chapter.

At the same time any examination of education systems in, for example, the UK and North America tells us that this is a time of turbulence as a result of centrally imposed changes. A consequence of this turbulence is a strong desire to keep schools stable. Stability is often achieved by remaining quiet in the eye of the storm that rages around education. Indeed a common theme in our interviews in the area of mentoring and school development confirms this view. There was a strong desire to not 'rock the boat'. There were implications here for the recognition of the potential for school development that partnerships with higher education might offer. Rocking the boat in the context of our study would have been to develop the role of mentor, and more particularly the demands of school-based training, beyond that which was safely contained in the mentor–student relationship. Development of the mentor role and a more complete integration of school-based training into the development priorities of schools would, it was feared, have destabilized existing roles, responsibilities and, above all, relationships.

For many classroom practitioners there has been simply too much change. The impact of too much change is twofold. First it can mean that any new initiatives are held lightly by a school because no doubt another new initiative will soon follow. Secondly, one result of not seizing new initiatives with enthusiasm is that schools don't make major changes in order to accommodate the new initiatives. The lack of deep engagement with the initiatives that come from outside the school means that school-based training may not achieve the potential for school development that we would argue it has. As one participant in our study, in this case a secondary school mentor, put it, 'This [mentoring role] could be truly transformational if only the hierarchy would take it seriously!' As Goodlad (1990) suggested, perhaps 'we must expand our thinking'.

## A fresh look at training relationships

Let us try to follow the advice of Goodlad and consider possible ways of perceiving the relationship between students, mentors, schools and universities. Goodlad's suggestion can be placed within a view of organizational development which allows us to begin to see the relationship between attending to the needs of students and at the same time maximizing benefits to schools.

Senge (1990), in his study of organizational development, argues that 'ways of seeing' in organizations are self-perpetuating and continue because alternatives are not easily recognized. He offers a useful framework for understanding what a learning organization might look like (Senge, 1994). He does not suggest that such an organization is easily achieved, but claims it can be recognized by the processes it exhibits. He defines these as five 'learning disciplines . . . which are lifelong programs of study and practice' (1994: 6). The emphasis on continuous development aimed at common educational goals is important in schools. Hopkins *et al.* (1994), in their overview of school improvement studies, identify much that is in common with the ideas of Senge we shall discuss in this chapter.

The five learning disciplines described by Senge (1994) are summarized as follows. The emphasis on process is, for us, their most important feature.

- *Personal mastery:* the expansion of our own capacities in order to create the kind of organization in which learning and self-efficacy are givens.
- *Mental models:* the development and reality checking of the frameworks with which we examine the world and from which we plan future actions.
- *Shared vision:* the creation of a sense of group commitment to an image of the future that is to be shared; and to the principles and guiding practices that will assist in its achievement.
- *Team learning:* the transformation of the conversational and collective thinking abilities of participants so that cooperation results in a collective ability that is greater than the sum of the contributions of individuals.
- *Systems thinking:* the analysis of the interrelationships and dynamics that give shape to particular organizational structures and procedures.

Elements of the first four of the disciplines just listed have been picked up in previous chapters of this book and will be revisited in Chapter 11. We shall therefore turn to the final discipline of systems thinking in this chapter. Senge identifies this discipline as the one that 'helps us to see how to change systems . . . and to act more in tune with the larger processes of the natural and economic world' (1994: 7).

A strong feature of Senge's analysis is that organizations become constrained by their own histories. When difficulties occur, the response is often the 'quick fix' which is little more than a repair or patching of the system. If this analogy is applied to schools, one can easily see a system under pressure constantly coping with more and more and straining at the seams. Fullan's observations of projectitis and resistance would confirm this view. It may be that, rather than seeing an enhanced involvement in initial teacher training as just another initiative, it would be timely to look afresh at the systems of schools and universities that connect in order to provide training for students and to reconsider relationships and dynamics within and between them.

Senge comments forcefully on the shackles of history that bind systems into practices that do not help them address future demands on them. He suggests as a consequence that systems need to be levered into change and that change does not easily arrive from the development of existing practices. He therefore proposes that organizations may benefit from what he calls *metanoia or a radical shift of mind*. Interestingly, the original sense of metanoia is repentance or a major turn from the old life to the new (Edwards and Collison, 1995b).

How might that leverage occur in the systems involved in providing training for students? Perhaps more importantly, what are the implications of any radical shift of mind for the organizations concerned? We shall start by looking at three types of training relationship.

## Type 1

A type 1 relationship is a familiar one and is little more than an extension of the traditional relationship that existed between a student and the classteacher who provided a site for student learning, together with helpful advice on how to teach. In this type of relationship, mentors are the pivots on which the relationships between schools and universities rest. The mentor may be a senior mentor with responsibility for several students and with a communication function with a number of other teachers who are hosting these students in their classrooms and mentoring their teaching. Nevertheless the initial training of teaching in the school is contained within the relationships that exist between those who are mentors and their students. Disruption to the school is kept to a minimum and the students are encouraged to 'fit in'.

This was the type of relationship that we observed to some degree in all the schools we visited in the study. This state of affairs is hardly surprising and we are certainly not offering a criticism of the schools that bravely but cautiously broke new ground by entering the training partnership we were observing. Rather we are pointing out the essentially conservative nature of the relationships we observed and the pivotal role of individual mentors in maintaining relationships between schools and universities.

One consequence of what we observed was that students and mentors often remained desert-islanded in their schools with little connection to the wider experiences that might be available and with little support for individual mentors within their own schools. The model is highly individual in its focus; consequently any leverage for change would have to be applied to individual mentors. We would argue that the strains of projectitis mean that individual mentors do not offer robust sites for leverage for change.

## Type 2

A type 2 model of mentoring and development represents an important step forward. In this model, the focus shifts from the learning of the student alone to the learning of the student, the mentor and university tutor through, for example, an expectation that mentors and tutors will attend to their own continuing professional development while involved in a training programme. A partnership programme based at the University of Reading and outlined by McCulloch (1993) attempts to achieve this.

The Reading initiative was given direction by a proposal of Adelman's (1989) that a process of practitioner research should operate at every level of education. The strategies employed by the Reading initiative are openness, collaboration, joint learning and risk-taking within a network that supports these features. McCulloch argues that the aim of the initiative is the individual enlightenment of all participants. It is this emphasis solely on the development of an individual that is, we suggest, the weakness of the initiative.

The application of leverage for change to individuals at every level in the programme certainly overcomes the limitations of expecting change to occur through the abilities of individual mentors to effect change in their own institutions. None the less, as we have argued elsewhere (Edwards and Collison, 1995b), there remains the danger that however supportive the network between individuals in different organizations might be, those individuals are open to marginalization in their own institutions. They are perhaps as likely to find themselves desert-islanded as the individual mentors we described in the type 1 training relationship.

*Type 3*

A type 3 relationship certainly represents a radical shift of mind. In this model, leverage for change is applied at the institutional level. It heeds Goodson's warning (1993) that a focus on practice, even in teacher research, plays into the hands of the new right by trivializing teaching into a set of routine activities. Consequently this view of a training partnership takes a wider organizational development perspective. The approach to change also goes further than simply school improvement and places schools and university departments of education as learning organizations within a framework that attends to Senge's suggestion that systems should be more in tune with the 'larger processes' of the wider world.

The shift of mind that is proposed in a type 3 relationship starts from a view of education as lifelong learning which is given coherence by continuous collaboration and discussion between all providers. At the root of this perspective is the suggestion that formal education systems would benefit from working with a consistent and coherent set of priorities which are constantly tested in theory and practice by all participants. Evidence of the shift of mind that is being indicated here would be, for example, collaboration in development planning between schools and university departments of education which attended to strategic planning, professional development and quality assurance in both sets of organizations and, for example, involved subject leaders or curriculum coordinators.

We would argue that partnerships of this kind could be, to quote the mentor we referred to earlier, 'truly transformational'. Their major strengths would lie in the fact that leverage for change was being applied to robust elements of the organizations concerned and not to individuals. In addition, both of the organizations that comprised the interlocking system of initial teacher training would be attempting to react coherently and simultaneously to a shared set of concerns. Importantly for both types of organization, those concerns would go wider that merely the learning of individual students.

## Dealing with resistance

In Chapter 1 we identified the stakeholders in the development of school-based teacher training and indicated the essentially conservative agenda they all shared. In this chapter we have begun to look more closely at the dynamics of relationships in schools and have suggested that the development of new roles and functions is difficult to achieve unless these meet priorities that are commonly recognized within a community of practice. During our three-year study of partnership in initial teacher training, we attempted to explore how schools were coping with the demands made upon them by their enhanced involvement in training students. We particularly wanted to discover ways in which schools were seeing any advantages that might come from such enhanced involvement (Edwards, 1994b; Edwards, 1995b).

Twenty colleagues in primary schools (ten head teachers and ten senior mentors) and ten colleagues in secondary schools (all of them subject mentors across the full national curriculum subject range) were interviewed. We found that schools wanted two things from students. These were that they should 'fit in' to the school and that they should bring fresh ideas into the school. We have explored in Chapter 3 how the students in primary schools dealt with these apparently conflicting demands by politely offering their tasks for children as gifts for their mentor hosts. We found very little evidence to suggest that schools were expanding their thinking to regard school-based training as anything other than an extension of existing practices.

We then explored, with the same colleagues, the impact of the contexts provided by schools as organizations on the development of the roles of mentors. We were particularly interested in finding out the extent to which schools were integrating the new mentor roles in initial training into the relationships and dynamics that made up each school as an organization.

A key to understanding how the role of mentor in each school was being allowed to develop was the way in which each of the mentors we interviewed accounted for their own success as a mentor. From this small sample of 20 mentors and ten head teachers, five coherent accounts emerged. We are not suggesting that these are the only ways of accounting for success as a mentor, but they are the accounts that we heard.

*I am already a bit special.* Mentors who accounted for success in this way mentioned, for example, that they had been advisory teachers or had previously worked with higher education. They were all teachers in primary schools. They did not feel that they had changed as a result of being a mentor and did not feel that they were having any impact on their schools as a result of their new roles.

*Now I have recognized it is a management role like any other, I am coping.* Mentors who fell into this group were in their second year of mentoring and were likely in their first year to have reported considerable role strain in ways that indicated that they were 'being torn in two' by the sense of responsibility to both their pupils and their students. Again these were all primary school mentors. In this case they were working in schools that had well-established systems for the development of new roles which enabled them to cope with the changing priorities that faced them annually. These mentors delegated some of the mentoring role in specific subject areas to curriculum coordinators and were planning clear programmes for the students. They felt that they had learnt a great deal from being a mentor but the mentor role was often simply one of several they were carrying.

*I am always there for the students, I am their friend and confidant.* Mentors in this group were mainly from primary schools and were becoming worn out by the demands of mentoring. They were not developing themselves professionally and were apparently getting no support from their schools. Like the 'bit special' group, they were desert-islanded with their students, but unlike them had not created a professional, teacherly distance between themselves and the students they were mentoring.

*I have always been a good supervisor and nothing has changed.* These mentors were all secondary school teachers. Quite rightly they assumed that they had been asked to be mentors because of their successful record on earlier non-partnership programmes. They were simply pleased that their contribution was being recognized by some form of remission from teaching. They did not appear to have changed their sense of themselves as professional by assuming an enhanced role in teacher training and their new role did not seem to be having any impact on the role dynamics that operated in their schools.

*This could be truly transformational but it isn't, thank goodness, for my subject.* We have already identified the frustrations felt by this group as a result of what they perceived to be the inability of senior management teams to take on this particular initiative with the seriousness these mentors felt it warranted. They were all teachers in secondary schools, who were able to take refuge in the common interest in the subject to be taught which they were able to share with the students they mentored. Again there was little evidence of the schools adjusting to the demands and possibilities offered by involvement in initial teacher training.

Of the five types of self-warranting accounts that we found in the interviews, only one seemed to suggest that schools were making adjustments to the new roles that were being assumed. The account that did indicate that organizational adjustments were being made was the one that claimed mentoring was a management role like any other. None of the accounts suggested that schools were making the kinds of adjustments that might indicate that some expansion of thinking about initial teacher training had occurred. And why should that expansion have occurred? The vision was not being offered by the university on which these partnerships were centred. Again there were sound reasons for this lack of vision, not the least of which is the complex set of funding arrangements in which initial teacher training and continuing professional development find themselves.

It appeared therefore that mentors and schools were dealing with the soundly-based resistance to change evident from a variety of directions by, in fact, not changing. However, not only were schools not making the most of any possibilities for school and professional development that might come from a rethinking of teacher education, they were also not offering the students anything that was greatly different from the school experiences that students might have received before the partnerships were put into place.

## School-based training: a new vision

So what might a transformed training relationship actually look like? Professional Development Schools (PDS) can give us some indication. A product of an attempt to develop the quality of elementary and high school provision in the USA, these schools are based on partnerships between schools, universities and school districts. The agenda for these schools was set by the Holmes Group. The agenda focuses on both initial training and continuing professional development. Schools have found that they have to do that within a context of constant and short-term accountability which is all too familiar to UK schools. As a result the agenda has proved to be complex and demanding for schools.

The evaluation of the creation of one such school (Grossman, 1992) presented by Fullan (1993) indicates that many of the problems we have identified in our study are a part of the change process associated with PDS. Fullan quotes Grossman's analysis that 'the teachers' feelings of being overwhelmed by change efforts reflects their sense of fragmentation, rather than their progression towards a single coherent goal' (p. 126). The lack of a single coherent goal seems to come from the difficulties experienced in pulling together career-long professional development and an initial teacher training programme in order to meet short-term performance indicators at the same time as recreating the school as a site for long-term professional learning.

Grossman's evaluation also suggests that the university side of the development partnership was not as well developed as it might have been. Grossman points out that, in our terms, leverage in universities has been at the level of individuals: a type 2 relationship. He states that 'the professional development centre has been cast as the on-going concern of relatively few faculty [members], rather than the responsibility of the college as a whole' (Fullan, 1993: 126). Fullan concludes his analysis of the evaluations of the early PDS by stating that PDS should be assessed by the extent to which they establish learning conditions for all educators. Importantly these conditions should bring about changes in the cultures of both schools and university departments of education.

Let us attempt to build a picture of what those changed cultures might look like. Leverage for change at the organizational level, or more specifically at the systems level, would allow for planned change which addresses the priorities of each organization. At the same time continual discussion between all practitioners, wherever they are positioned in the community of practice that is primary education, should allow for necessary flexibility within the broad planning framework.

The creation of a broad planning framework would, for example, allow an extension of the useful practice that we observed in a few schools where mentors involved curriculum coordinators in work with students and where students were included in school-based in-service training sessions. An extension of these activities would be the planned involvement of university tutors in a school's staff development programme in ways that also meshed with the anticipated learning needs of students.

Quality control of the student experience could be placed more firmly with primary schools if students' training goals could be shared and schools enabled to deal with the needs of mentors that emerged from evaluations of the students' experiences. The development of schools as sites for the professional learning of staff would be an element in the schools' ability to respond to concerns that arise from students' and mentors' evaluations of their experiences in schools. We have evidence, from the initial training programme for secondary school teachers that we mentioned earlier in this chapter, that some secondary schools are indeed assuming an effective role in the quality control of the student experience in partnership with their university collaborator.

Universities and schools could collaborate in ways that build on the research and development consultancies in which some higher education tutors are involved. These may focus on the development of subject-specific teaching. The first author has, for example, worked with schools in one local education authority over the past three years in the supportive evaluation of curriculum development in the areas of literacy and numeracy in primary schools.

The focus of development may also be more directly related to pedagogy, for example, ways of dealing with 4-year-old learners. Or it may be useful for colleagues to work together in the design and introduction of anti-bullying policies or increased parental involvement in the literacy support of their children at home. The idea of a community of practice helps us to see how practitioners who are based in higher education may have something valid to offer those who are based in schools.

The reverse is also true; that experience of testing out existing ideas and experiencing those that emerge in practice is an important part of the professional development of higher education staff. While we have focused here on the impact of our proposals on schools, we do not wish to underemphasize the impact on higher education that our suggestions might have, were they to be adopted. The areas where any culture change would be observed would include the erosion of boundaries between in-service and pre-service provision and definitions of research that took into account its impact on practice in schools.

But we do not have a history of radical change in Britain; ours is a much more evolutionary culture. It is one more marked by pragmatic adaptation than by the five disciplines outlined by Senge (1994). What signs are there that pragmatic adaptation may move us towards the vision we have just attempted to share? The framework for the inspection of initial teacher training in operation at the time of writing (late 1995) gives clear indication that the ideas we are proposing would, in some form, benefit student teachers.

The framework informs us that subject leaders are to play a significant part in the school-based training of students. This emphasis is unsurprising given current concerns over the state of subject teaching in primary schools. In Chapter 6 we identified the transformation of subject knowledge into tasks aimed at supporting the learning of students as a major challenge for primary teacher training. The inspection framework also states that students need to be involved in the wider purposes of the school and particularly they have to work with colleagues in the processes of development planning. Desert-islanding of student and mentor is certainly not encouraged by either of these training demands on schools.

The considerable attention paid to management and quality assurance in the inspection framework also reflects a view that indicates that quality assurance is at the core of training partnerships. The central position of effective management and quality assurance in the framework suggests that quality assurance and its management have to be joint ventures. Consequently training partnerships have to be seen as more than simply another initiative for schools in which they assume the role of providers of sites for training.

We would argue that it is in the interests of schools to heed the ideas that are evident in the inspection framework. The way forward would be to develop the idea, evident in our data, of being a training site for student teachers. The development might overtly take on the expectation that schools become more clearly sites for the training of staff. The staff concerned may be newly qualified teachers; experienced practitioners whose training needs are identified in appraisals; practitioners who wish to develop in ways that support school development planning; or indeed head teachers. Recent indications that professional development profiles will become a feature of the professional lives of teachers would suggest that a learning school would be likely to recruit learning staff.

The opportunities for work-based learning for professionals that are promoted by, for example, the Management Charter Initiative and the National Council for Vocational Qualifications suggest that the proposed emphasis on schools as sites for the learning of professionals is not extraordinary.

However our suggestion that the creation of learning schools occurs in partnership with higher education in order to ensure a coherent and soundly researched programme of professional development is perhaps a little more than a recognition of the importance of work-based learning. We are in fact placing considerable emphasis on the knowledge base of teaching and how it may be developed and articulated in partnerships between schools and universities. We turn to that topic in Chapter 11.

## Further reading

A collection of papers that picks up a number of current primary school development concerns is Southworth, G. (ed.) (1994) *Readings in Primary School Development*, London, Falmer. It includes chapters on school improvement (Weindling, also Ainscow and Hopkins); inspection (Southworth and Fielding); collaboration (Hayes) and INSET (Dadds).

The relationship between teacher development and school-based development activities, in this case a curriculum development project, is analysed in the next paper in ways that bring together understandings of teachers' learning and school development. Day, C. (1990) The development of teachers' personal practical knowledge through school-based curriculum development projects, in C. Day, M. Pope and P. Denicolo (eds) *Insight into Teachers' Thinking and Practice*, London, Falmer. A paper in a different collection – Kelly, M., Beck, T. and Thomas, J. (1992) Mentoring as a staff development activity, in M. Wilkin (ed.) *Mentoring in Schools*, London, Kogan Page – specifically explores the staff development potential in mentoring.

Ann Lieberman has written extensively on the rationale for the development of professional cultures in schools in North America. Lieberman, A. (ed.) (1988) *Building a Professional Culture in Schools*, New York, Teachers College Press. Also Lieberman, A. and Miller, L. (1990) Teacher development in professional practice schools, *Teachers College Record*, 92: 105–22.

Andy Hargreaves and David Hartley both provide food for thought in their analyses of postmodernity and the problems the condition has brought for teacher education. Hargreaves, A. (1993) Teacher development in the postmodern age: dead certainties, safe simulation and the boundless self, in P. Gilroy and M. Smith (eds) *International Analyses of Teacher Education*, Abingdon, Carfax; Hartley, D. (1993) Confusion in teacher education: a postmodern condition? in the same volume.

# MAKING THE MOST

# OF RELATIONSHIPS

# WITH HIGHER

# EDUCATION

## Who are the players?

In our discussion of Professional Development Schools (PDS) in the previous chapter, we saw that these schools were usually established as the result of partnerships between schools, universities and school districts which were set at the general improvement of education provision. The PDS were seen as part of a common enterprise aimed at a shared set of goals even though interests and priorities were slightly different for each of the participants. An interesting gap in any UK attempt at establishing similar arrangements is the reduction in influence of the UK equivalent to school districts. Until the late 1980s local education authorities had an important broker function to play and many were actively bringing together schools and higher education in ways that were beneficial for both groups. When the brokers disappeared, higher education found itself without right of entry into schools and with only market forces to rely on as a system for maintaining what had often been valuable connections between the two phases of education (Edwards, 1991).

The reality was that market forces in the period that followed all too often led to the kind of quick fixes that Senge observed and we discussed in Chapter 10 (Senge, 1990; 1994). Quick fixes were bound to be seen to be the best option given the pressure of the changes that schools were coping with and the decline in funding available to them in recent years. However, a purchaser–provider model of relationships between schools and higher education now seems to operate even when partnerships in initial training exist (Edwards and Collison, 1995b). It can be seen in initial teacher training when schools see themselves as providing sites for student training which are purchased by universities and in INSET when schools purchase places on training provision offered by higher education.

The situation we have just outlined does not seem to fit that easily with the ideas of a community of practice which we have been exploring throughout the book. The purchaser–provider model of relationships certainly makes dialogues between higher education and schools much less spontaneous than they were and, we suggest, increases the likelihood of the separation of theory and practice. As we shall argue later, this has perhaps more immediately damaging implications for theory. However, impoverished theory will eventually impact on practice.

While schools and higher education are key players in the relationship we are discussing, students also have an important part to play. We talked in the last chapter about the desert-islanding of mentors and their students in the midst of busy schools. However, another feature of the changing relationships between schools and higher education in the training of teachers is the vulnerable position of students as they attempt to move between the two environments in partnership training programmes. The reduction in time available to higher education for supporting students in school has meant that tutor visits have been greatly reduced, with an impact on the role of students in maintaining relationships between schools and higher education. Students, in partnership programmes at least, can be now seen as quite isolated links between the schools in which they practise and their higher education bases. Of course a number of partnership programmes have recognized the potential vulnerability of students and have built student peer support systems into the design of their training courses.

One function that higher education tutors were able to fulfil when they were frequent visitors to students in school was to help the students translate instances of practice into quite broad principles for the development of practice. Tutors were therefore able to be bridges between the well-researched knowledge base of teaching and the practice in which that knowledge was used and developed. This translation service was an important one and one emphasized for example in the work of Rogoff *et al.* (1984). Writing generally about learning, they argue that learners are assisted by those who create bridges between contexts, draw analogies and channel their learning.

Without the support of tutors as bridge builders, it becomes increasingly difficult for students to bring together theory and practice. Unless, of course, this begins to happen when principles of practice are highlighted in mentoring conversations and connected to understandings in operation in the public domain in seminars.

It may be that students feel that they are required to speak different languages in the settings of schools and universities and to be the translators themselves. If this is the case, and there is certainly an interesting research study in the hypothesis, then theory and practice are yet further separated as theory is not explored from the starting point of practice and not likely to be tested knowingly in practice.

As important players in the relationship between schools and higher education, the students have a relatively short life. We would argue that investment in students as links between the two bases produces only short-term gains and places considerable pressures on the students. It also allows students to play one base against the other! All the partnership programmes with which we are familiar have recognized the difficulties we have just outlined and have established link tutor systems in which a university tutor creates strong relationships with a limited number of schools and works closely with staff in those schools as they support the learning of the students who are placed there. In this chapter we want to pursue how these relationships might be built upon to the benefit of all the players.

While we shall be focusing particularly on relationships that occur within training partnerships, we think that the ideas we shall be discussing could equally easily be accommodated by school-centred training schemes in primary schools. What is required is what Senge (1994) described as 'shared vision'. The vision we want to share is one of a community of developing practice where both schools and university departments of education work together on the common enterprise of the development of provision.

## Training relationships

Another of Senge's 'five learning disciplines' listed in the previous chapter is 'team learning'. In this area of organizational learning, he places great emphasis on the development of conversational skills that in turn enhance the thinking and understanding of team members. We have stressed the importance of dialogues between mentors and students and between mentors themselves throughout the book. Now we want to explore how university staff might be included more directly in these conversations.

Our own experience suggests that conversations between mentors and tutors which are focused on students and their practice are what can be termed 'real conversations', conducted between professionals of equal standing around a common concern. Indeed, tutors are highly dependent on mentors for maintaining the quality of students' experience and very much value the support that mentors give students. Importantly, these conversations invariably occur in schools, and tutors are working from less information than are the mentors as they discuss student behaviour. If there is any imbalance of power in these conversations, it is in favour of the mentors.

The relationships between link tutors and mentors that might develop out of these conversations seem to be fertile ground for the development of relationships in other aspects of professional life. Mentors are increasingly invited to talk to students on higher education-based elements of courses, teachers are involved in admissions interviews for teacher training programmes and in the design and validation of professional training programmes. However all of this appears very much a one-way flow, from school to higher education. We have found little evidence of an equivalent counter-flow from universities to schools.

Part of the problem lies in one of the difficulties brought out in the evaluation of the PDS initiative which we discussed in the previous chapter. Partnership relationships with universities are usually only with the university staff who are concerned with initial teacher training. These are often different people from those who specialize in continuing professional development and school improvement consultancies. Even if they are not different people, the funding arrangements for higher education are often taken to determine a separation of a great deal of pre- and in-service work. The separation is not an insoluble problem for higher education. It is also very much in its interests to find a solution. At least one university has started to 'reperceive' its relationship with schools by renaming its in-service department its 'partnership department' and by bringing school-based training and what was formerly INSET under one management system.

What does a department of education have to offer that might be of use to schools? When we have discussed these ideas with teacher colleagues, they have emphasized the importance of the easy availability of higher education staff who also get to know the school well and become useful sounding boards for school staff. Once in that position, if the individual tutor does not have the specific expertise required for the development work that the school wants doing, she or he will know a colleague who has. When this happens, the gap left by the loss of the LEA broker role is filled by stronger direct links between individual schools and university departments. Universities therefore also have much to gain.

There is a lot of adult learning now going on in schools. At the time of writing the training of newly qualified teachers (NQTs) is well established and the introduction of the Headlamp programme for newly appointed head teachers is under way. There is also every indication that professional development profiling will continue throughout a teacher's career.

Profiles may be based on simplistic models of competence in which attention is given only to final performance and ignores the learning on which it is based. On the other hand, if the profiles were to follow the model offered by the National Council for Vocational Qualifications (NCVQ) (Jessup, 1991), attention to the knowledge base of the final performance would be a feature of evidence of competence. Other professional groups, for example psychologists, are creating their post-qualification professional development profiles along NCVQ lines (BPS, 1995). It would be ironic if the teaching profession were to adopt a competence framework for continuing professional development that did not attend to the knowledge base which is a precursor to competent performance.

Much but not all of the learning that leads to post-qualification competence would, if the experience of other professional groups is to be learnt from, in most cases best occur in the workplace. The advantages would be particularly evident in situations where teachers may be gently supported into full participation in the practices that they want to develop. Developing an understanding of practice while developing practice would seem to overcome the twin failings of dissemination and transfer which have so bedevilled in-service education. Let us however explore that claim through a specific example.

A current priority in primary schooling in the UK is to find ways of meeting the subject knowledge needs of children at the top end of Key Stage 2 (10- and 11-year-olds). The contribution that might be made by higher education subject-specialist tutors from departments of education is perhaps obvious here. The options for forms of collaboration include the teaming of school subject leaders with university subject tutors to develop subject-based curriculum policies suited to partnership schools, to support curriculum development initiatives, to provide school-based INSET sessions and to work alongside colleagues in classrooms.

If other performance indicators are to be met by the partners in this development work, then school-based staff could find that their work could be accredited for university-validated continuing professional development awards. Equally the development work undertaken by tutors in partnership with teacher colleagues may be treated in researcherly ways that lead to the publications that they require for their own academic credibility. We would argue that all educational research has to develop out of and be developed in aspects of educational practice. So we now turn to research relationships.

## Research relationships

Another of Senge's 'learning disciplines' (Senge, 1994) was the use of 'mental models'. These, he claimed, need to be continually reflected upon in order to improve and clarify the intellectual frameworks with which we make sense of our worlds. In Chapter 9 we suggested that an action research framework can be used both for the development of mentor practice and for enabling informed discussions between students and their mentors on aspects of practice. We now want to consider how research relationships may be developed between university-based tutors and school-based teachers in ways that are likely to develop the educational understandings of both sets of participants.

Our framework for that exploration is of course the sharing and testing of meanings which come from the dialogues that occur while participating together as members of a community of practice. We have consistently argued that primary specialists who are based in higher education are legitimate members of the community of practice that is primary education. In order for them to participate usefully, their particular contribution to the development of understanding and expertise in the community has to be recognized. We suggest that their role lies in their contribution to the development and clarification of 'best fit' mental models. They cannot, of course, do this meaningfully alone. Mental models that do not fit the reality experienced in schools are less than useful and arguably even dangerous.

The separation of theory and practice has been a theme in this book and we shall not labour it much further here. However, one of the reasons behind our enthusiasm for some partnership models of training is the potential that exists within them for the development of educational theory from an informed analysis of practice. Neither teachers nor university tutors can easily do that in isolation from each other.

However, more practical justifications for partnerships in research may need to be offered. We shall take for granted that, if we are suggesting in Chapter 9 that students will learn a great deal from focused enquiries which are then discussed with mentors, then qualified staff will also learn a great deal from being involved in a similar set of processes at their own levels of professional development, with support from, perhaps, universities. We shall therefore focus only on how partnerships in research may impact on quality assurance systems in schools and on how appraisal might operate. In both cases we shall look at research as evaluation.

The relationship between school development planning and evaluation has been long recognized and presented with clarity by, for example, Elliott (1991) and Hargreaves and Hopkins (1991). They emphasize how involvement in the evaluation of developments can help teachers to gain ownership of the changes being evaluated and adapt them appropriately. Higher education staff can be of considerable help here. As an evaluator of development initiatives, the first author finds herself involved frequently in conversations in schools in which the goals of specific developments are clarified, the strategies and timescales planned and ways of identifying and measuring desired process and outcomes created. The conversational process is one that seems to work well. Simply telling teacher colleagues how to approach evaluation in in-service sessions seems to be far less effective.

As a follow-up to the conversations, higher education tutors with experience of evaluation can support colleagues in classrooms as they develop reliable but non-intrusive ways of collecting the outcome measures that are demanded by those who have funded the development initiatives. Also, once higher education staff establish relationships with schools that enable schools to evaluate effectively for themselves, schools will be better placed to be equal partners in the quality assurance of initial training programmes than is perhaps currently the case for the majority of programmes.

The action research framework outlined in Chapter 9 has, in the past, also had some impact on appraisal systems. In these approaches to appraisal, individual teachers have been encouraged to focus on a particular element of practice and to consider ways of developing it. The appraiser then adopts the role of critical friend in teasing out understandings and implications of the practice that has been observed. To our knowledge these approaches to appraisal fell by the wayside because of the training costs involved in preparing staff for working with action research frameworks and methods. Once again there is a role for higher education tutors in supporting the development of school staff. Because of the often sensitive nature of the appraisal process, there is a lot to be said for working with a member of a university education department who knows the school and the particular demands that it makes on staff.

## Relationships in the development of practice

This set of relationships takes us to Senge's concern with the development of 'personal mastery' (Senge, 1994). He defines this as an interrelationship between person and context. Pursuit of personal mastery is seen in the expansion of our personal capacity 'to create the results we most desire' and in the creation of an environment 'which encourages all its members to develop themselves toward the goals and purposes they choose'. In Chapter 10 we considered in some detail the importance of a sense of personal effectiveness and the need for an environment that encouraged that. One of the problems with staff development which aims specifically at the development of practice, but is delivered away from the workplace, is that it cannot easily take into account the environmental barriers to change that classteachers often meet when they return to school.

The big advantage for schools of building on relationships established with link tutors, and therefore with university departments of education, is that support for the development of practice can take into account the constraints and opportunities for development that are peculiar to each school. Members of the school community can be moved gently and appropriately to confident use of the desired practices. One important feature of Senge's definition of personal mastery is its developmental approach. He talks of learning to expand our personal capacity to get where we want to get to.

This is very different from a transfer or dissemination model of professional learning where the success of dissemination or of transfer of information or skills may be assessed on a simple 'can do–cannot do' check-list. Senge's framework is much more in tune with a view of the construction and testing of knowledge in a community of practice and the idea of a discourse of practice in which we are able to assume positions as legitimate peripheral participants as we learn within it. (See Chapter 2.) Taking this view, we recognize that to begin with we may assume quite marginal positions in an element of practice and only gradually with assistance move towards 'the goals and purposes (we) choose' (Senge, 1994). Such a view of staff development, however, demands the continuous availability of assistance for school staff as they tentatively try out new practices. It also perhaps therefore demands a revision of the roles of higher education tutors as they work with schools.

## The faculty friend

We seem to be suggesting that schools would benefit from nurturing a relationship with a friendly member of an education faculty. Relationships between schools and universities do, however, have to be more firmly based at the institutional level than the faculty friend suggestion would indicate. As we argued in Chapter 10, we need to heed Senge's advice that we sometimes cannot move forward fruitfully by simply extending existing practices. Rather we have to apply his fifth learning discipline of 'systems thinking' and reperceive relationships between the two types of institution.

Creating stronger institutional links between schools and university departments of education could allow the developments we have outlined to be worked out without putting excessive strain on the role of link tutors, or faculty friends as they have just been relabelled. These links would have considerable advantages for higher education. Payment arrangements would allow some recycling of funding for initial teacher training back to universities in ways that would allow higher education to maintain the curriculum-specialist staffing it requires.

The loss of the subject-specialist staffing base from university education departments as a result of an enhanced initial training role for schools would have eventual ramifications for the schools. A simple example would be the demise of maths education teams. We would argue that their specialist educational knowledge could not be replaced by advice from tutors from mathematics departments in universities who are not experts in the pedagogy of the subject for school-age children. We are clearly advocating the need to think holistically about education and the quality of provision for pupils, students and practitioners, wherever they are based.

## Key features of sound relationships between schools and universities

Senge's frameworks lead us to consider both structures and processes, but the emphasis is clearly on processes. The structural changes we have been discussing may be difficult to achieve to any extensive degree, though we would argue that they are important. It has certainly been proved possible, in at least one university in England, to effect some changes in internal organization and funding arrangements between schools and higher education. These have enabled staff to work towards the relationships that exhibit the openness and trust that we have been suggesting.

What then might be the key features of a mutually supportive relationship between a school and a university department of education? This is our list. We would imagine that schools might want to adjust it to their own experiences.

- Easy access for school staff to the school's faculty friend.
- Easy access to classrooms and other parts of the school for a faculty friend.
- Open talk between school and faculty staff which allows exploration of differences as well as common concerns.
- Mutual respect for what each practitioner has to offer to the development of understandings in the community of practice.
- No definition of who is the *real practitioner* if the definition excludes other practitioners.
- An understanding of the difficulties and opportunities which partners face in their places of work.
- A commitment to the joint development and open critique of education and its value base.

It does appear that it would be difficult to achieve these features in a relationship that was based on a purchaser–provider model. One element of such a model is, of course, the idea that all that schools are doing, when they accept a greater responsibility for initial training, is providing a site for student trial and error learning. The active mentors we have been advocating are also the learning professionals who are operating in support systems that assist their professional development. We recognize that what we are suggesting presents a major challenge for universities and that tutors will have to earn their places in the community of practice we have been discussing.

## Articulating the knowledge base of teaching

Teaching in primary schools is a difficult and complex job. Its very unpredictability elevates it beyond any idea that it is simply a set of skills that can be learnt in practice. The fluency of the knowledge in action of expert practitioners may belie the complexity of the underpinning of skilled teachers' intelligent actions. Yet as we have argued earlier, the amalgam of the knowledge base of teachers is rarely articulated effectively by teachers themselves.

One outcome of the lack of commonly shared and teacher-articulated definition of the knowledge that underpins practice in schools is that the knowledge base is all too easily dismissed by those outside education. The danger from this silence about pedagogy is particularly strong in the area of early years practice, where it is more difficult to discuss curriculum content knowledge as a justification for regarding teaching as a profession. Nevertheless, the lack of emphasis on an articulation of the complex principles of pedagogy can be seen at times to threaten the professional status of all primary school teachers.

One major effect of allowing university-based primary specialists legitimate involvement in the community of practice of primary teaching is the role they can play in developing a coherent view of pedagogy that can be effectively communicated by all concerned.

## Further reading

Two papers in McBride, R. (ed.) (1993) *Teacher Education Policy: Some Issues Arising from Research and Practice*, London, Falmer, pick up and elaborate some of the points we have been attempting to make in this chapter. The chapter by Bridges presents a considered case for the continuing involvement of universities in teacher education and emphasizes the need to either maintain the conditions for engagement with ideas or risk the general impoverishment of education. The chapter by Schostak is an interesting vision of what a wider view of education might look like.

Bridges, D. and Kerry, T. (eds) (1993) *Developing Teachers Professionally: Reflections for Initial and Inservice Trainers*, London, Routledge, is an interesting collection of papers which argues from a range of perspectives for collaboration between all who are involved in the creative development of teacher education.

Becher, T. (ed.) (1994) *Governments and Professional Education*, Buckingham, Open University Press/SRHE, is a collection of papers which allow the reader to place changes in the profession of teaching and in teacher education, in the wider context of developments in professions and in other European countries.

Hargreaves, A. (1994) *Changing Teachers: Changing Times*, London, Cassell, is a stimulating read that calls into question a number of easily held assumptions about the profession of teaching.

# ENDPIECE

## Contexts

The importance of contexts for learning has been a theme in this book. In our discussions of these contexts we have tried to do two things. First, we have examined ways in which learners may be inducted into understandings of the meanings that are held and developed in the community of practice of primary education. Secondly, we have argued that an analysis of practice is an insufficient basis for the training of beginning teachers. Consequently, learning situations at times need to be contrived and informed by information available in the public domain and students need at times to be positioned as learners in schools.

Whether learning opportunities arise naturally in classroom settings or are contrived by expert practitioners, they are shaped by current understandings held within a community of practice. Following Lave and Wenger (1991), we have argued that learning can be re-defined as gaining mastery of current social and cultural practices, in this case the practices of being a primary school teacher. At the same time we have suggested that, unless these practices are open to continual scrutiny and consequent development, learning will be limited and the improvement of practice and its contexts less likely.

Learning is not therefore something that students do in isolation as a result of being given access to sites for trial and error attempts at mastery. Rather learners are positioned within a set of social processes which constitute what is to be learnt and the mastery of which represents learning.

Learning to be a teacher consequently needs to be placed in wider understandings of policy, school improvement and staff development.

## The political context of teacher education

We have made little of UK national teacher education policy in the text. But it cannot be ignored. Indeed we would suggest that it has much in common with policy directions in other countries, and consequently should not be ignored (Gilroy and Smith, 1993). The very fact that a craft knowledge view of teaching is being pursued in UK government policy (Gilroy, Price, Stones and Thornton, 1995) indicates that any discussion of how to prepare beginning teachers is itself a political statement. We quite clearly do not see teaching as the application of a set of simple skills that can be acquired and shaped in practice. For us, teaching is a complex process which demands an induction into its complexity and the recognition of teaching as a profession.

Consequently we have been exploring ways of developing thinking practitioners who will consider their own practices. However, thinking practitioners will do more than that. They will, as they develop as professionals, be able to set their professional decisions for scrutiny alongside the practice of more expert practitioners and against suggestions that are available in the research literature. While the text has drawn on a study of initial teacher training, we hope that much of what we have said is of relevance to induction programmes as they too attempt to develop thinking practitioners.

Thinking practitioners are unlikely to take any context for granted. Rather they will feel able to question its purposes. In initial teacher training that questioning may be focused on school-related matters, for example the treatment of parents, gendered practices, or opportunities for combating racism. Later the questioning cast of mind can be turned to wider policy issues and the development of the profession at a time of quite widespread deprofessionalization, in the UK at least.

## The school context of teacher education

Creating contexts for learning has been one theme in the book and in Chapters 10 and 11 we emphasized the importance of learning schools as contexts for the professional development of all the adults who work with children in them. We have stressed that initial teacher training should neither operate on a simple money-led, purchaser–provider model of training, nor be regarded as a form of colonization by higher education. Relationships in initial training have changed and, we hope, will continue to do so. Consequently it is timely that all involved in education should consider education as a continuum that runs from nursery provision to continuing professional development. We are all players on the same team and need to learn to work together for the benefit of pupils.

We have particularly emphasized how higher education tutors and researchers need to be recognized as legitimate participants in what we have described as the community of practice that is primary education. The advantages for schools, we suggest, come from what higher education tutors might be able to offer as schools develop the contexts for learning opportunities that they provide. The advantages for higher education and for education generally are that theory in the field of education can, in part at least, arise from observation of practice and can be tested in practice. However, higher education will have to make adjustments and earn its place in the community.

## The classroom context of teacher education

Most of the data we have discussed have been collected in classrooms and have drawn attention to the ways that mentors can assist the learning of students as they work in classrooms and plan for and evaluate that work. However, we have emphasized that this is only part of the story and there are weaknesses in any training system that isolates mentor and students and focuses solely on that relationship in students' experiences of being in schools.

Training to be a thinking professional demands more than reflection on practice. It needs opportunities for the consideration of wider professional issues and the creation of a cast of mind which regards initial training as the start of a long process of professional development. We have suggested that one of the major challenges for teacher trainers has been the need to alert students to the demands and complexities of being a teacher and to shift their preconceptions of primary teaching brought from their own experiences as pupils before the age of 11. These changes need to be managed without reducing students' abilities to work confidently in the dreadfully public arenas that are classrooms.

Mentoring is therefore not simply the provision of situations where students can pick up craft knowledge. It is an active process and requires mentors to consider students as another set of learners in their classrooms. If primary school teaching is complex, mentoring simply adds to the complexity.

## Concluding points

We are grateful to the schools and individual mentors who cooperated with us in this study of the early days of partnership between schools and higher education. We are aware that schools dealt differently with the demands and rewards of involvement in the partnership scheme we studied. Consequently we return to the point we made in Chapter 1, where we stated that mentoring is a developing concept and that we believed that mentors and the schools in which they work should play their part in the contesting and development of what school-based training can be. We hope that this book has provided a starting point for consideration of at least some aspects of what is involved in learning to teach in primary schools and how expert teachers might support that learning.

We hope too that our emphasis on dialogue throughout the book means that enhanced involvement in initial teacher training provides an opportunity for wider professional dialogues between all of us who see ourselves as members of the community of practice that is primary education.

## Further reading

The current political context of education in England and Wales is interrogated from the perspective of policy sociology by Stephen Ball in Ball, S. J. (1994) *Education Reform*, Buckingham, Open University Press.

Maguire, M. (1995) Dilemmas in teaching teachers: the tutor's perspective, *Teachers and Teaching: theory and practice*, 1(1): 119–31 reminds us of the complexities of the work involved in preparing teachers.

# REFERENCES

Adelman, C. (1989) The practical ethic takes priority over methodology, in W. Carr (ed.) *Quality in Teaching*. London: Falmer.

Alexander, R. (1995) *Versions of Primary Education*. London: Routledge.

Anning, A. (ed.) (1995) *A National Curriculum for the Early Years*. Buckingham: Open University Press.

Aubrey, C. (ed.) (1994) *The Role of Subject Knowledge in the Early Years of Schooling*. London: Falmer.

Ball, S. J. (1994) *Education Reform*. Buckingham: Open University Press.

Bassey, M. (1995) *Creating Education Through Research*. Kirklington: Kirklington Moor Press in association with the British Educational Research Association. (Available from BERA, 15 St John's Street, Edinburgh.)

Becher, T. (ed.) (1994) *Governments and Professional Education*. Buckingham: Open University Press/SRHE.

Bennett, N. and Cass, A. (1988) The effects of group composition on group interactive process and pupil understanding, *British Educational Research Journal*, 15(1): 19–40.

Bennett, N., Desforges, C., Cockburn, A. and Wilkinson, B. (1984) *The Quality of Pupil Learning Experiences*. London: LEA.

Bennett, N. and Dunne, E. (1992) *Managing Classroom Groups*. Hemel Hempstead: Simon and Schuster.

Bourne, J. (ed.) (1994) *Thinking Through Primary Practice*. London: Routledge.

Bridges, D. and Kerry, T. (eds) (1993) *Developing Teachers Professionally: Reflections for Initial and Inservice Trainers*. London: Routledge.

British Psychological Society (BPS) (1995) personal communication.

Calderhead, J. (1988) The development of knowledge structures in learning to teach, in J. Calderhead (ed.) *Teachers' Professional Learning*. London: Falmer.

Calderhead, J. and Gates, P. (eds) (1993) *Conceptualising Reflection in Teacher Development.* London: Falmer.

Carraher, T., Carraher, D. and Schliemann, A. (1990) Mathematics in streets and in schools, in P. Light, S. Sheldon and M. Woodhead (eds) *Learning to Think.* London: Routledge.

Carter, K. (1992) Creating cases for the development of teacher knowledge, in T. Russell and H. Munby (eds) *Teachers and Teaching: From Classroom to Reflection.* London: Falmer.

Chaiklin, S. and Lave, J. (eds) (1993) *Understanding Practice: Perspectives on Activity and Context* Cambridge: CUP.

Clandenin, J. and Connelly, M. (1986) The reflective practitioner and the practitioners' narrative unities, *Canadian Journal of Education*, 11(2): 184–98.

Clark, C. M. and Yinger, R. J. (1987) Teacher planning, in J. Calderhead (ed.) *Exploring Teachers' Thinking.* London: Cassell.

Clayden, E., Desforges, C., Mills, C. and Rawson, W. (1994) Authentic activity and learning, *British Journal of Educational Studies*, 42(2): 163–73.

Collison, J. (1994) The impact of primary school practices on student learning in the classroom. Paper presented at the British Educational Research Association Annual Conference: Oxford.

Collison, J. (1995) How mentors support student teachers in the application of subject knowledge in the classroom. Paper presented at the European Conference on Educational Research: Bath.

Collison, J. and Edwards, A. (1994) How teachers support student learning, in I. Reid, H. Constable and R. Griffiths (eds) *Teacher Education Reform: the Research Evidence.* London: Paul Chapman.

Crossman, L., Dean, M., Owen, P. and Webb, D. (1995) 'The literacy log', unpublished teaching material, University College of St Martin, Lancaster.

Day, C. (1990) The development of teachers' personal practical knowledge through school-based curriculum development projects, in C. Day, M. Pope and P. Denicolo (eds) *Insight into Teachers' Thinking and Practice.* London: Falmer.

Department for Education (DFE) (1993) *The Initial Training Of Primary Teachers: New Criteria for Courses.* DFE Circular No. 14/93. London: HMSO.

Desforges, C. (1985) Matching tasks to pupils' attainment, in N. Bennett and C. Desforges (eds) *Recent Advances in Classroom Research.* Edinburgh: Scottish Academic Press.

Doyle, W. (1986) Classroom organisation and management, in M. C. Wittrock (ed.) *Handbook of Research on Teaching.* New York: Macmillan.

Dreyfus, H. L. and Dreyfus, S. E. (1986) *Mind Over Machine: the Power of Human Intuition and Expertise in the Era of the Computer.* Oxford: Blackwell.

Edwards, A. (1991) Teacher education and local authorities: jointly constructing a future for education, *Local Government Policy Making*, 18(1): 33–8.

Edwards, A. (1994a) Curricular applications of classroom groups, in P. Kutnick and C. Rogers (eds) *Groups in Schools.* London: Cassell.

Edwards, A. (1994b) The impact of involvement in ITT on processes and procedures in schools: alternative narratives. Paper presented at the British Educational Research Association Annual Conference: Oxford.

Edwards, A. (1995a) Teacher education: partnerships in pedagogy?, *Teaching and Teacher Education*, 11(6): 595–610.

Edwards, A. (1995b) Possibilities for the development of mentor identity. Paper presented at the conference of the International Study Association of Teacher Thinking: St Catherine's, Ontario.

Edwards, A. (1996) Can action research give coherence to the school-based learning experiences of students? in C. O'Hanlon (ed.) *Professional Development Through Research in International Settings*. London: Falmer.

Edwards, A. (in press) Guests bearing gifts: the position of student teachers in primary school classrooms, *British Educational Research Journal.*

Edwards, A. and Collison, J. (1995a) What do teacher-mentors tell student-teachers about pupil learning in primary schools?, *Teachers and Teaching: theory and practice*, 1(2): 265–79.

Edwards, A. and Collison, J. (1995b) Partnerships in school-based teacher training: a new vision? in R. McBride (ed.) *Teacher Education Policy: Some Issues Arising from Research and Practice*. London: Falmer.

Edwards, A. and Knight, P. (1994) *Effective Early Years Education*. Buckingham: Open University Press.

Edwards, A. and Knight, P. (eds) (1995) *Assessing Competence in Higher Education*. London: Kogan Page.

Edwards, A. and Talbot, R. (1994) *The Hard-Pressed Researcher*. London: Longman.

Edwards, A. and Twiselton, S. (1995) Competences in the classroom: what happens to learning? Paper presented at the Sixth European Conference for Research on Learning and Instruction: Nijmegen, the Netherlands.

Elliott, B. and Calderhead, J. (1993) Mentoring for teacher development: possibilities and caveats, in D. McIntyre, H. Hagger and M. Wilkin (eds) *Mentoring: Perspectives on School-Based Teacher Education*. London: Kogan Page.

Elliott, J. (1991) *Action Research for Educational Change*. Buckingham: Open University Press.

Eraut, M. (1994) *Developing Educational Knowledge and Competence*. London: Falmer.

Eraut, M. (1995) Schön shock: a case for reframing reflection-in-action? *Teachers and Teaching: theory and practice*, 1(1): 9–22.

Fullan, M. (1991) *The New Meaning of Educational Change*. London: Cassell.

Fullan, M. (1993) *Change Forces: Probing the Depths of Educational Reform*. London: Falmer.

Furlong, J., Hirst, P., Pocklington, K. and Miles, S. (1988) *Initial Teacher Training and the Role of the School*. Buckingham: Open University Press.

Furlong, J. and Maynard, T. (1995) *Mentoring Student Teachers*. London: Routledge.

Gibbs, G. (1992) Improving the quality of student learning through course design, in R. Barnett (ed.) *Learning to Effect*. Buckingham: Open University Press/SRHE.

Gilligan, C. (1982) *In a Different Voice*. Cambridge, MA: Harvard University Press.

Gilroy, P. (1993) Reflections on Schön: an epistemological critique and a practical alternative, in P. Gilroy and M. Smith (eds) *International Analyses of Teacher Education*. Abingdon: Carfax.

Gilroy, P., Price, C., Stones, E. and Thornton, M. (1994) Teacher education in Britain: a JET symposium with politicians, *Journal of Education for Teaching*, 20(3): 261–301.

Gilroy, P. and Smith, M. (eds) (1993) *International Analyses of Teacher Education*. Abingdon: Carfax.

Gipps, C. (1994) *Beyond Testing: Towards a Theory*. London: Falmer.

Goodlad, J. (1990) *Teachers for our Nation's Schools*. San Francisco: Jossey-Bass.

Goodson, I. (1993) Forms of knowledge and teacher education, in P. Gilroy and M. Smith (eds) *International Analyses of Teacher Education*. Abingdon: Carfax.

Grossman, P. (1992) In pursuit of a dual agenda: creating a middle level professional development school, in L. Darling-Hammond (ed.) *Professional Development Schools: Schools for Developing a Profession*. New York: Teachers College Press.

Hargreaves, A. (1993) Teacher development in the postmodern age: dead certainties, safe simulation and the boundless self, in P. Gilroy and M. Smith (eds) *International Analyses of Teacher Education*. Abingdon: Carfax.

Hargreaves, A. (1994) *Changing Teachers: Changing Times*. London: Cassell.

Hargreaves, D. and Hopkins, D. (1991) *The Empowered School*. London: Cassell.

Harré, R. (1983) *Personal Being*. Oxford: Blackwell.

Hartley, D. (1993) Confusion in teacher education: a postmodern condition? in P. Gilroy and M. Smith (eds) *International Analyses of Teacher Education*. Abingdon: Carfax.

Harvard, G. and Hodkinson, P. (eds) (1994) *Action and Reflection in Teacher Education*. Norwood: Ablex.

Holmes Group (1990) *Tomorrow's Schools*. East Lansing, MI: Holmes Group.

Hopkins, D. (1993) *A Teacher's Guide to Classroom Research*, 2nd edn. Buckingham: Open University Press.

Hopkins, D., Ainscow, M. and West, M. (1994) *School Improvement in an Era of Change*. London: Cassell.

Huberman, M. (1995) Networks that alter teaching: conceptualisations, exchanges and experiments, *Teachers and Teaching: theory and practice*, 1(2): 193–211.

Jessup, G. (1991) *Outcomes: NVQs and the Emerging Model of Education and Training*. London: Falmer.

John, P. (1995a) Understanding the apprenticeship of observation in initial teacher education: exploring student teachers' implicit theories of teaching and learning, in G. Claxton, T. Atkinson, M. Osborn and M. Wallace (eds) *Liberating the Learner: Lessons for Professional Development in Education*. London: Routledge.

John, P. (1995b) The supervisory process in teacher education: learning event or learning bind? in G. Claxton, T. Atkinson, M. Osborn and M. Wallace (eds) *Liberating the Learner; Lessons for Professional Development in Education*. London: Routledge.

Johnson, D. W. and Johnson, F. (1994) *Joining Together: Group Theory and Group Skills*, 4th edn. Englewood Cliffs, NJ: Prentice Hall.

Karmiloff-Smith, A. (1992) *Beyond Modularity*. Cambridge, MA: MIT Press.

Kelly, M., Beck, T. and ap Thomas, J. (1992) Mentoring as a staff development activity, in M. Wilkin (ed.) *Mentoring in Schools*. London: Kogan Page.

Kohlberg, L. (1975) The cognitive development approach to moral education, *Phi Delta Kappa*, 56: 670–7.

Kutnick, P. and Rogers, C. (eds) (1994) *Groups in School*. London: Cassell.

Lave, J. (1993) The practice of learning, in S. Chaiklin and J. Lave (eds) *Understanding Practice: Perspectives on Activity and Context*. Cambridge: CUP.

Lave, J. and Wenger, E. (1991) *Situated Learning: Legitimate Peripheral Participation*. Cambridge: CUP.

Levine, H. (1993) Context and scaffolding in developmental studies of mother–child problem-solving dyads, in S. Chaiklin and J. Lave (eds) *Understanding Practice: Perspectives on Activity and Context*. Cambridge: CUP.

Lieberman, A. (ed.) (1988) *Building a Professional Culture in Schools*. New York: Teachers College Press.

Lieberman, A. and Miller, L. (1990) Teacher development in professional practice schools, *Teachers College Record*, 92: 105–22.

Light, P. and Littlejohn, K. (1994) Cognitive approaches to group work, in P. Kutnick and C. Rogers (eds) *Groups in School*. London: Cassell.

Maguire, M. (1995) Dilemmas in teaching teachers: the tutor's perspective, *Teachers and Teaching: theory and practice*, 1(1): 119–31.

Maynard, T. (1996) Mentoring subject knowledge in the primary school, in D. McIntyre and H. Hagger (eds) *Mentors in Schools: Developing the Profession of Teaching*. London: David Fulton.

Maynard, T. and Furlong, J. (1993) Learning to teach and models of mentoring, in D. McIntyre, H. Hagger and M. Wilkin (eds) *Mentoring: Perspectives on School-Based Teacher Education*. London: Kogan Page.

McBride, R. (ed.) (1995) *Teacher Education Policy: Some Issues Arising from Research and Practice*. London: Falmer.

McCulloch, M. (1993) Democratisation of teacher education: new forms of partnership for school-based teacher education, in P. Gilroy and M. Smith (eds) *International Analyses of Teacher Education*. Abingdon: Carfax.

McIntyre, D., Hagger, H. and Wilkin, M. (eds) (1993) *Mentoring: Perspectives on School-Based Teacher Education*. London: Kogan Page.

McNamara, D. (1994) Subject study in teacher education, in G. Harvard and P. Hodkinson (eds) *Action and Reflection in Teacher Education*. Norwood: Ablex.

Mercer, N. (1995) *The Guided Construction of Knowledge: Talk Amongst Teachers and Learners*. Clevedon: Multilingual Matters.

Miller, J. (1990) *Creating Spaces and Finding Voices*. New York: SUNY.

Morris, P. (ed.) (1994) *The Bakhtin Reader*. London: Edward Arnold.

Mosley, J. (1991) *All Round Success: Practical Ideas to Enhance the Self-Esteem of Children in the Primary School*. Trowbridge: Wiltshire County Council.

Murphy, P., Selinger, M., Bourne, J. and Briggs, M. (eds) (1995) *Subject Learning in the Primary Curriculum: Issues in English, Science and Mathematics*. London: Routledge in association with the Open University.

Nias, J. and Groundwater-Smith, S. (eds) (1988) *The Enquiring Teacher: Supporting and Sustaining Teacher Research*. London: Falmer.

Norman, D. A. (1978) Notes towards a complex theory of learning, in A. M. Lesgold, J. W. Pellegrino, S. D. Fokkema and R. Glaser (eds) *Cognitive Psychology and Instruction*. New York: Plenum.

Phillips, T. (1985) Beyond lipservice: discourse development after the age of nine, in G. Wells and J. Nicholls (eds) *Language and Learning: an Instructional Perspective*. London: Falmer.

Pollard, A., Broadfoot, P., Croll, P. and Abbott, D. (1994) *Changing English Primary Schools? The Impact of the Education Reform Act at Key Stage One*. London: Cassell.

Proctor, A., Entwistle, M., Judge, B. and Mckenzie-Murdoch, S. (1995) *Learning to Teach in the Primary Classroom*. London: Routledge.

Reid, I., Constable, H. and Griffiths, R. (eds) (1994) *Teacher Education Reform: Current Research*. London: Paul Chapman.

Resmick, L., Levine, J. and Teasley, S. (eds) (1993) *Socially Shared Cognition*. Washington, DC: APA.

Riggs, A. and Hayhurst, A.-M. (1995), personal communication.

Rodd, M. (1995) Dimensions of mathematics mentoring in school-based initial teacher education, *Teachers and Teaching: theory and practice*, 1(2): 229–46.

Rogoff, B., Gauvain, M. and Ellis, S. (1984) Development viewed in its cultural context, in M. Bornstein and M. Lamb (eds) *Developmental Psychology: an Advanced Textbook*. Hillsdale, NJ: LEA.

Russell, T. and Munby, H. (1991) Reframing: the role of experience in developing teachers' professional knowledge, in D. Schön (ed.) *The Reflective Turn*. New York: Teachers College Press.

Schön, D. A. (1987) *Educating the Reflective Practitioner*. San Francisco: Jossey-Bass.

Schunk, D. H. and Meece, J. L. (eds) (1992) *Student Perceptions in the Classroom*. Hillsdale, NJ: LEA.

Senge, P. (1990) *The Fifth Discipline: the Art and Practice of the Learning Organisation*. New York: Doubleday.

Senge, P. (1994) *The Fifth Discipline Fieldbook*. New York: Doubleday.

Shulman, L. (1987) Knowledge and the foundations of the new reform, *Harvard Educational Review*, 57: 1–21.

Slavin, R. (1990) Cooperative learning, in C. Rogers and P. Kutnick (eds) *The Social Psychology of the Primary School*. London: Routledge.

Southworth, G. (ed.) (1994) *Readings in Primary School Development*. London: Falmer.

Sylva, K., Roy, C. and Painter, M. (1980) *Childwatching at Playgroup and Nursery School*. Oxford: Grant McIntyre.

Tharp, R. and Gallimore, R. (1988) *Rousing Minds to Life*. Cambridge: CUP.

Tomlinson, P. (1995) *Understanding Mentoring*. Buckingham: Open University Press.

Tomlinson, P. and Saunders, S. (1995) The current possibilities for competence profiling in teacher education, in A. Edwards and P. Knight (eds) *Assessing Competence in Higher Education*. London: Kogan Page.

Torrance, H. (1994) *Authentic Assessment*. Buckingham: Open University Press.

Wertsch, J., Del Rio, P. and Alvarez, A. (eds) (1995) Sociocultural Studies of Mind. Cambridge: CUP.

Wilkin, M. (ed.) (1992) *Mentoring in Schools*. London: Kogan Page.

Wilkin, M. (1995) The environment. Opening address at Illuminating Mentoring Seminar, SRHE Mentoring Network: London.

Wolf, A. (1995) *Competence-Based Assessment*. Buckingham: Open University Press.

Wood, D. (1986) Aspects of teaching and learning, in M. Richards and P. Light (eds) *Children of Social Worlds*. Oxford: Polity Press.

Wood, D., Bruner, J. S. and Ross, G. (1976) The role of tutoring in problem-solving, *Journal of Child Psychology and Psychiatry*, 17: 89–100.

Wood, D. and Middleton, D. (1975) A study of assisted problem-solving, *British Journal of Psychology*, 66: 181–91.

Woods, P. (ed.) *Contemporary Issues in Teaching and Learning*. London: Routledge in association with the Open University.

Yeomans, R. and Sampson, J. (eds) (1995) *Mentoring in the Primary School*. London: Falmer.

Yinger, R. and Hendricks-Lee, M. (1993) Working knowledge in teaching, in C. Day, J. Calderhead and P. Denicolo (eds) *Research on Teacher Thinking: Understanding Professional Development*. London: Falmer.

# INDEX

**UNDERSTANDING MENTORING**
REFLECTIVE STRATEGIES FOR SCHOOL-BASED TEACHER PREPARATION

**Peter Tomlinson**

The current move to school-based mentoring offers the possibility of considerable improvement over traditional arrangements for initial teacher preparation. But this opportunity will only be realized if old assumptions about theory and practice are modified and new practices based on a better understanding of ways in which effective teaching may be acquired. Starting from the assumption that practising teachers already possess many resources relevant to mentoring, *Understanding Mentoring* offers practical strategies and programmes for mentoring in the context of recent work on intelligent skill development, professional thinking and learning, counselling and helping strategies, and the nature and assessment of teaching competence. It should therefore be a useful resource for teachers taking on a mentoring role, and for those engaged in training and academic courses on school-based teacher education.

*Contents*
*School-based teacher education: opportunity and challenge – Learning teaching: a framework for understanding mentoring – The reflective coach: functions and forms of mentoring – The effective facilitator: interpersonal aspects of mentoring – Classroom strategies and their learning potential – Classroom strategies and their pupil management potential – Teacher competence profiling for student assessment and development – Mentoring in practice: coaching tactics – Mentoring in practice: student programmes and organizational issues – Appendix – References – Index.*

256pp     0 335 19306 4 (paperback)

# EDUCATING THE WHOLE CHILD
## CROSS-CURRICULAR SKILLS, THEMES AND DIMENSIONS
### John and Iram Siraj-Blatchford (eds)

This book approaches the 'delivery' of the cross-curricular skills, themes and dimensions from a perspective emphasizing the culture of primary schools and the social worlds of children. The authors argue that the teaching of skills, attitudes, concepts and knowledge to young children should not be seen as separate or alternative objectives, but rather as complementary and essential elements of the educational process. It is the teacher's role to help children develop and build upon the understandings, skills, knowledge and attitudes which they bring with them into school. Learning for young children is a social activity where new skills and understandings are gained through interaction with both adults and with their peers. Each of the approaches outlined in the book is thus grounded in an essential respect and empathy for children and childhood as a distinct stage in life and not merely a preparation for the world of adulthood. For instance, the authors argue that responsibilities and decision making are everyday experiences for children and that they need to be able to develop attitudes and skills which enable them to participate fully in their own social world.

### Contents
*Cross-curricular skills, themes and dimensions: an introduction – Little citizens: helping children to help each other – Effective schooling for all: the 'special educational needs' dimension – Racial equality education: identity, curriculum and pedagogy – 'Girls don't do bricks': gender and sexuality in the primary classroom – Children in an economic world: young children learning in a consumerist and post-industrial society – Catching them young: careers education in the primary years – Understanding environmental education for the primary classroom – Health education in the primary school: back to basics? – The place of PSE in the primary school – Index.*

### Contributors
John Bennett, Debra Costley, Debbie Epstein, Peter Lang, Val Millman, Lina Patel, Alistair Ross, Ann Sinclair Taylor, Iram Siraj-Blatchford, John Siraj-Blatchford, Balbir Kaur Sohal, Janice Wale.

192pp     0 335 19444 3 (paperback)     0 335 19445 1 (hardback)

# CREATIVE TEACHERS IN PRIMARY SCHOOLS

## Peter Woods

Is creative teaching still possible in English schools? Can teachers maintain and promote their own interests and beliefs as well as deliver a prescribed National Curriculum?

This book explores creative teachers' attempts to pursue *their* brand of teaching despite the changes. Peter Woods has discovered a range of strategies and adaptations to this end among such teachers, including resisting change which runs counter to their own values; appropriating the National Curriculum within their own ethos; enhancing their role through the use of others; and enriching their work through the National Curriculum to provide quality learning experiences. If all else fails, such teachers remove themselves from the system and take their creativity elsewhere. A strong theme of self-determination runs through these experiences.

While acknowledging hard realities, the book is ultimately optimistic, and a tribute to the dedication and inspiration of primary teachers.

The book makes and important contribution to educational theory, showing a range of responses to intensification as well as providing many detailed examples of collaborative research methods.

### Contents
*Introduction: Adapting to intensification – Resisting through collaboration: A whole-school perspective of the National Curriculum – The creative use and defence of space: Appropriation through the environment – The charisma of the critical other: Enhancing the role of the teacher – Teaching, and researching the teaching of, a history topic: An experiment in collaboration – Managing marginality: Aspects of the career of a primary school head – Self-determination among primary school teachers – References – Index.*

208pp     0 335 19313 7 (paperback)     0 335 19314 5 (hardback)